Y0-AAV-902

MELVILLE AND AUTHORITY

by Nicholas Canaday, Jr.

UNIVERSITY OF FLORIDA PRESS / GAINESVILLE, 1968

EDITORIAL COMMITTEE

Humanities Monographs

T. WALTER HERBERT, *Chairman*
Professor of English

G. PAUL MOORE
Professor of Speech

CHARLES W. MORRIS
Professor of Philosophy

REID POOLE
Professor of Music

C. A. ROBERTSON
Professor Emeritus of English

MELVIN E. VALK
Professor of German

AUBREY L. WILLIAMS
Professor of English

AS
36
.F58
NO.28

LIBRARY
UNIVERSITY OF MIAMI

COPYRIGHT © 1968 BY THE BOARD OF
COMMISSIONERS OF STATE INSTITUTIONS
OF FLORIDA

LIBRARY OF CONGRESS
CATALOG CARD NO. 68-65060

PRINTED BY THE STORTER PRINTING COMPANY
GAINESVILLE, FLORIDA

PREFACE

The question arose in my mind whether a long life spent in subordination to external authority might have resulted in a dominant theme in Melville's fiction. From the day he stepped aboard a merchantman until he left the customhouse some fifty years later, Herman Melville felt the galling shackles of restraint. Seldom throughout the voyage of his life did he feel free to steer his own course—to captain his own ship. Always a common sailor on shipboard, he experienced from an early age the harsh discipline of the sea. In the South Seas he deserted his ship to escape the restricted life in the forecastle. These experiences forcibly taught the lesson of the chain of authority. "Who ain't a slave?" asked Ishmael, and he answered, "However the old sea-captains may order me about . . . I have the satisfaction of knowing that it is all right, that everybody else is one way or other served in much the same way."

This study tests the extent to which the theme of authority appears in Melville's works through 1851. Each work is examined in the order of original publication so that it is possible to see the development of the theme and its increasing importance in Melville's thought until it culminates in *Moby-Dick*. In Melville's later years the theme becomes more diffuse, though the relevance of "Benito Cereno," for example, much of *Clarel*, and *Billy Budd* as a kind of recapitulation, will be evident.

The term *authority* is here used to mean the power, vested by the warrant of moral right or legal right, in persons or groups, which coerces those subject to it in the spheres of belief and action. Authority cannot function—although it may exist—without power. Alternatively, the coerciveness of power may be based upon force operating without authority. Authority implies right, but there is a latent ambiguity in the term *right*: it may mean "that which is warranted by moral approval" or "a power vested by law or custom" (*Black's Law Dictionary*, 4th ed., 1951). It will be seen that Melville explored these and other complexities inherent in the concept of authority and man's response to it. Several kinds of authority—including the authority of state and church, the ship captain, parents, society, and God—make up Melville's unifying theme that this study will test.

The Constable Edition (1922-24) has been used as the most convenient source for the text of the early romances and novels while we are awaiting the Northwestern-Newberry Edition. For the text of *Moby-Dick* the Hendricks House Edition, edited by Luther S. Mansfield and Howard P. Vincent (New York, 1952), has been used. Citations to these editions are included in parentheses in the text of this study.

An earlier version of Chapter I has appeared as "The Theme of Authority in Melville's *Typee* and *Omoo*," University of Houston *Forum*, IV (Fall, 1963), 38-41. I wish to express grateful appreciation to Professor Harry Warfel, who directed my doctoral dissertation, of which this monograph is an outgrowth, at the University of Florida; and to the Graduate Research Council of Louisiana State University, which provided a grant to afford the author the opportunity to put this study in its present form for publication.

CONTENTS

1. A FROLICSOME ADVENTURE

In spite of the fact that Melville's first two published works received more acclaim during his lifetime than any of the others, *Typee* (1846) and *Omoo* (1847) are often regarded by scholars as mere travel books, somehow only preliminary to the important body of his work. For many it is the midpoint of *Mardi* (1849) that marks the beginning of Melville's growth as an artist. For others, the record in these early romances of Melville's Polynesian experience represents only a "first phase of disillusionment,"[1] the "extremes of good and evil in human life,"[2] or a "defense of the Noble Savage and a eulogy of his happy life."[3] Of central importance in both books, however, is the theme of authority—specifically the coercing power of legal right or an assumed moral right and the tension created by rebellion against it.

Typee, Melville's first published book, is an episodic romance of the South Seas based upon his adventures in the Marquesas Islands, where he deserted from the whaling ship *Acushnet* in 1842. Ostensibly *Typee* has as its primary purpose the presentation of an authentic glimpse of Polynesian life, but within this travel-book framework ideas are suggested, and sometimes overtly presented, that are to be of concern to Melville throughout his career as a writer. The emphasis is on the adventure, the peep at Polynesian life. If in addition his Pacific journey and exposure to a primitive society confirmed him in the art of constructing symbols,[4] the achievement of such an art is not yet realized. If another lesson of Polynesia is that its life is "an archaic level of

1. Lawrance Thompson, *Melville's Quarrel With God* (Princeton, 1952), p. 54.
2. Ronald Mason, *The Spirit Above the Dust* (London, 1951), p. 36.
3. Charles R. Anderson, *Melville in the South Seas* (New York, 1939), p. 178.
4. James Baird, *Ishmael: A Study of the Symbolic Mode in Primitivism* (New York, 1960), p. 94.

1

existence which wears the mask of childhood and innocence but is really guilty of terrible crimes and which in its devious ways traps unwary voyagers,"[5] such a lesson is revealed mostly by a kind of restless wariness on the part of the narrator. If modern man, in spite of his longing, would soon be bored with the innocence and idyllic delight of the Typee valley,[6] this idea too is no more than implied in the book. *Typee* explores the problem of authority more overtly than it does these ideas, but Melville did not yet make use of symbols to suggest the implications of his narrative or to crystallize his ideas. Instead, this major theme is presented in terms of the structure of the narrative and by the author's intrusion of his comments into the story through his narrator.[7]

In the first place, the fictional pattern of the dissatisfied sailor who deserts his ship to escape a tyrannical captain— a pattern that reappears throughout Melville's writing—is established early in *Typee*. The brief episode concerning Captain Vangs of the whaling ship *Dolly* indicates that from the beginning Melville was vitally concerned with the authority of the ship's master and particularly the abuse of it.[8]

5. Richard Chase, *Herman Melville* (New York, 1949), p. 32.

6. Robert Stanton, "*Typee* and Milton: Paradise Well Lost," *Modern Language Notes*, LXXIV (1959), 411.

7. It will become apparent that the conclusions reached in my study are somewhat different from those of John Bernstein, *Pacifism and Rebellion in the Writings of Herman Melville* (The Hague, 1964). Bernstein's approach in the early novels parallels mine in broad outline: "As seen in *Mardi*, pacifism would seem to include a belief in Christianity and faith in the essential order of the universe, a concern for the individual man, and an acceptance of man's weaknesses and limitations. Rebellion consists of a defiance of any or all powers stronger than man, an interest often with ideals rather than people, and a commitment to the cause of armed revolution as a means of social reform" (p. 56). In the later works, however, Bernstein treats rebellion more specifically as rebellion against injustice, and his conclusion (which I do not share) is that "perhaps the keynote to Melville as a writer and as a thinker, is his insistence that mankind is never more noble than in this struggle against injustice, both human and universal, that by rebelling against evil, man can wrest meaning from the cosmos and in this struggle find some sort of salvation" (pp. 220-21).

8. Although the various ship captains in Melville's works have identifiable real life counterparts whose names have been discovered, it is impossible to determine to what extent these captains were models for Melville's portraits. There is simply not enough evidence to distinguish

2

These are the narrator's reasons for deserting: "The usage on board of her was tyrannical; the sick had been inhumanly neglected; the provisions had been doled out in scanty allowance; and her cruises were unreasonably protracted. The captain was the author of these abuses; it was vain to think that he would either remedy them, or alter his conduct, which was arbitrary and violent in the extreme" (25). The narrator is confronted with the dilemma that faces all sailors in similar situations. He must either remain on the ship under intolerable conditions or he must rebel. It is true that the captain's authority is based upon law, and Melville recognized its legal limitations, but the impracticality of appealing to the courts while the ship is two or three years away from port is obvious. Desertion becomes the only source of relief. The tyrannical captain and the desertion of the narrator form a recurrent fictional pattern in Melville's works, later filled out with much more detail.

Secondly, the authority of church and state is presented in *Typee* under the general concept of the bringing of civilization to Polynesia. For the most part, Melville's description of native life deals with savages who have never been exposed to the civilizing effects of the white man; nevertheless, there are certain islands familiar to the narrator where European civilization has been imposed on the natives by occupying garrisons of troops, proselytizing missionaries, or visiting ships' crews. Wherever the narrator comments on this civilizing process, he sees the results as adverse. The French forces, which took over some of the Marquesas Islands in 1842, are described as bringing brutality and cruelty to the lives of the inhabitants. The "moral" pressures exerted by the churchmen, backed by the force of arms, result in the establishment of a standard of hypocrisy replacing the naïve simplicity of the islanders, and nominal Christianity carries disease, vice, and premature death in its wake. The various ships' crews

between what is drawn from life and what is free invention. The various captains are treated in many places, but as usual with such questions one must start with Jay Leyda's indispensable *The Melville Log*, 2 vols. (New York, 1951).

3

that go ashore after months at sea bring riot and debauchery to the islands. The narrator observes that the natives, "unsophisticated and confiding . . . are easily led into every vice," and he concludes that "were civilisation itself to be estimated by some of its results, it would seem perhaps better for what we call the barbarous part of the world to remain unchanged" (21). These remarks are interpolated into the narrative to protest the authority of a civilization that imposes unwanted and unneeded standards on an alien people.

The fact that the Marquesans lived in peace and harmony with the persuasion of custom serving as an adequate substitute for the coercion of formal authority probably most impressed Melville. Without a standard or general rule of conduct except for certain taboos, without laws, courts, or police, the islanders live together "with a harmony and smoothness unparalleled . . . in the most select, refined, and pious associations of mortals in Christendom" (269). Melville's narrator clearly approves the high degree of social order that has been achieved without the aid of formal law or law enforcement machinery: "The grand principles of virtue and honour, however they may be distorted by arbitrary codes, are the same all the world over. . . . It is to this indwelling, this universally diffused perception of what is *just* and *noble*, that the integrity of the Marquesans in their intercourse with each other is to be attributed" (270). But Melville was not always to hold the view that truth, justice, and the better principles of human nature would prevail without the aid of the statute book: "I will frankly declare, that after passing a few weeks in this valley of the Marquesas, I formed a higher estimate of human nature than I had ever before entertained. But alas! since then I have been one of the crew of a man-of-war, and the pent-up wickedness of five hundred men has nearly overturned all my previous theories" (273). For him the compelling attractiveness of Polynesia was based in large part upon the superfluous nature of the authority exercised there by church and state. *Typee*, remembered by the general reader chiefly because of its exotic locale,

4

forms an integral part of the development of Melville's thought.

Melville's narrative in *Omoo* is a continuation of the adventures described in *Typee*. Again the apparent purpose of *Omoo* is to portray the geography and inhabitants of a portion of the South Seas. In the case of *Omoo* there is an element added to the population: drifting ex-sailors of many nations who congregate at Tahiti. Again in the second book Melville depicts the presence of the white man as having a corrupting influence on the native population. Melville's narrator bitterly attacks the authority of church and state, which attempts to coerce the natives into a pattern of life alien to their nature. Missionaries have prohibited native games, dances, and festivals because of alleged immorality, but the vices of the white man, adopted and practiced in secrecy, are far more pernicious. As in *Typee*, Melville here views the state of nature as eminently more commendable than a forced conformity to European standards.

Rebellion against authority is implied in the structure of the entire narrative. The story presents an overt anti-authoritarianism in the sympathetic and enthusiastic account of the wanderings of the many beachcombers who rove the islands. These ex-sailors live an existence marked by their refusal to be coerced by any rules; they are deserters who have chosen to live by their wits outside the bounds of law. The title of the book is a clue to this important theme. "Omoo" in the Marquesan dialect, according to Melville, means a "rover," one who wanders from one island to another. The narrator indicates that he views with sympathy their desire to free themselves from the bonds of civilization. Their presence is, in fact, accepted by all who reach the islands. The ships' officers expect some sailors to jump ship as they reach port, and their replacements are recruited there before leaving. If the deserters are recaptured by their own officers, the punishment for desertion is never severe; if they manage to escape, the sailors simply sign on a new ship when they are ready to return to civilization. The matching of wits between the sailors and those in authority has become a kind of game with each side observing the rules. Before the whaling ship *Julia,* carrying Melville's sailor-narrator, reaches Tahiti, it stops at another small island to gather in some of its crew who had deserted there several months before. When these seamen are brought aboard, their tales of adventure on the island are eagerly received by the other members of the crew. Melville's narrator describes their desertion as a "frolicsome adventure" (27). It is in this spirit that the narrator and his friends desert in Tahiti. Soon the island constabulary confines them in the local jail, but the sailors know that if they can remain ashore until the *Julia* departs with another crew they will then be set free. Many choose never to return to civilization. The actions of these rovers in *Omoo* provide an element of anti-authoritarianism that is a principal theme in the book.

The specific theme of the authority of the ship captain is far more important in *Omoo* than in *Typee.* In *Omoo* three captains are portrayed in some detail, and the narrator's struggle with the first one extends for almost one-third of the book. Captain Guy of the whaler *Julia* is pictured as a very ineffectual commander whose weakness causes misery and dissension among his crew. The men all know his history: he had, "by some favouritism or other . . . procured the command of the vessel, though in no wise competent" (11). In *Typee* Melville had portrayed Captain Vangs of the *Dolly* as a tyrant, but in *Omoo* an ineffectual captain is the reason for deserting. The *Julia* has already lost almost half its crew by desertion when it reaches the Marquesas; and since many of the sailors still aboard are ill, or pretending to be ill, from long periods of dissipation in port, the work of manning the ship is inequitably distributed. Captain Guy has been too lenient in allowing shore leave during the cruise, and his belated attempt to prevent liberty in Tahiti makes matters worse. Furthermore, some of the men have secured access to the liquor stores during the voyage, and this group stays drunk most of the time, using their stolen bottles to purchase relief from duty from the other sailors. The captain observes the frequent disorder but fails to take corrective measures. Sailors actually sick are left unattended, and the chief mate, who is usually drunk, rules the crew by knocking them about. Since the chief mate's physical force provides the only semblance of discipline among the crew, the captain gives tacit approval to his methods. Some sailors retaliate physically, and the brawls below deck are frequent. Captain Guy ignores the disorder, although he knows that the crew refers to him as "The Cabin Boy" and "Paper Jack" (11). Melville demonstrates, by the chaos he pictures aboard the *Julia,* what happens when a ship captain cannot control his crew. When the ship approaches Tahiti, sixteen of its twenty sailors refuse to serve aboard any longer. Captain Guy calls on the consul ashore to help him restore order, but it is too late for outside help to be effective.

Two other captains appear rather prominently in *Omoo.* The captain of the French frigate *Reine Blanche,* who takes the deserters under his command for a few days in the harbor, is also faced with dissension among his crew. The poor quality of the rations and their short supply aboard the French ship account for part of the trouble. The principal cause of the unrest stems from the fact that this warship commander is a martinet. Too much of a disciplinarian, he makes a great show of his authority: in port his sailors are kept busy exercising yards and sails, maneuvering boats, manning battle stations, and firing guns. The French captain stands in contrast to Captain Guy of the *Julia,* but neither of them is wholly successful in his command.

A third captain, who appears at the very end of *Omoo,* seems to represent the mean between these two extremes, and he is the first and only ship captain favorably portrayed by Melville in these two romances dealing with seafaring men. This gentleman is the master of the whaler *Leviathan,* the ship which takes the narrator away from the islands at the end of the book. By that time Melville's spokesman is very cautious about choosing a captain to ship with, and he talks to some of the members of the *Leviathan*'s crew before approaching their master. To this captain's credit, he is the first ship's master seen in the islands who is not trying to recruit a crew; all his own sailors plan to sail with him when he leaves. The narrator takes this information as a favorable sign, is interviewed by the *Leviathan*'s commander, and is accepted as a seaman aboard the ship for the long voyage home.

The theme of authority in *Omoo* is far more central than in *Typee*. Both books contain comments on the adverse effects of European civilization—represented by the authority of church and state—on the Polynesians. In *Omoo* is added the element of anti-authoritarianism produced by the actions of the roving ex-seamen throughout the islands. These rovers are in constant protest against every type of authority that seeks to constrain them. They take advantage of the geographic location of the far-off islands of the South Pacific to desert their ships with impunity, because they know that the feared authority of maritime law is quite ineffective at such a distance. Melville also describes the command function of the ship captain more thoroughly in *Omoo* than in *Typee*, and in doing so he indicates what factors make for discipline or the lack of it. *Typee* and *Omoo* are books primarily written to describe a place, a populace, and a culture; but in the narrative line continuing through both books the theme of authority assumes an ever-increasing importance.

2. TAJI'S QUEST FOR AUTHORITY

When Melville's *Mardi* was published in 1849, it was immediately apparent that the book was not another *Typee* or *Omoo*. The first two romances recounted mostly without embellishment the author's experiences in the South Seas, but *Mardi* used the raw material of Polynesia for another purpose. Melville revealed in his letters to his English publisher John Murray in 1847 and 1848 that *Mardi* had become two books, because what started out to be another narrative of South Sea adventure became sometime during 1848 a romance "wild enough . . . & with a meaning too."[1] An examination of the structure of the book shows this division. The narrative begins with Melville's sailor-narrator west of the Galapagos Islands aboard the whaling ship *Arcturion*. In the mid-Pacific the narrator determines to jump ship and sail in an open boat west to the Kingsmill Chain (Gilbert Islands) some thousand miles away. He recruits another seaman, Jarl, to accompany him. They sail westward for sixteen days until they meet and board the derelict brigantine *Parki*, which carries them farther on their passage westward. They leave the *Parki* in a storm to continue their journey in an open boat, and nine days later they come upon a canoe bearing a beautiful blonde maiden, Yillah, who as a prisoner of some native priests "was being borne an offering from the island of Amma to the gods of Tedaidee" (I, 152). The narrator effects the rescue of the maiden, but in the process he kills the priest Aleema, who is in charge of the group. Bringing Yillah aboard his small craft, the narrator changes his plans. No longer interested in continuing to the Kingsmill Islands, he now decides to sail southward: ". . . what cared I now for the green groves and bright shore? Was not Yillah my shore and my

1. Melville to Murray, March 25, 1848. Merrell R. Davis and William H. Gilman, eds., *The Letters of Herman Melville* (New Haven, 1960), p. 71.

grove? my meadow, my mead, my soft shady vine, and my arbour? . . . Enough: no shore for me yet" (I, 168). As they voyage aimlessly southward, Yillah at last yearns for the shore. The narrator again turns westward and sights land the next morning. The sighting of land begins Chapter LII, significantly entitled "World Ho!" Not the Kingsmill Islands or any other charted islands of the Pacific have been sighted, but the fictional archipelago of Mardi.

Once Yillah, Jarl, and the narrator have landed on the Mardian island of Odo, the second part of the book begins. In Mardi the narrator becomes known as Taji, "a sort of half-and-half deity . . . ranking among their inferior ex-officio demi-gods" (I, 191). He and Yillah are together for a time in idyllic bliss, but soon the white maiden mysteriously disappears. King Media of Odo orders a search be made, but she is not found on his island. Taji announces his intention to leave the island to continue the search, and King Media proposes to accompany him. Joining the quest are three other natives: Mohi, a historian; Babbalanja, a philosopher; and Yoomy, a poet. With these four companions Taji searches for Yillah throughout the entire archipelago of Mardi.[2] Among the eighteen islands of Mardi that Taji either visits or hears described is discovered a great variety of institutions and customs, but Taji never again finds Yillah. The quest, of course, gives Melville ample opportunity for satire. In this sightseeing tour of the world, Taji, like Swift's Gulliver or Rabelais' Pantagruel, is a novice who is initiated into the peculiarities of each country visited.[3]

The broad chart of Melville's *Mardi* contains as many varied ideas as there are islands in the archipelago, but Taji's quest for the elusive Yillah forms the unifying theme. It is the

2. Jarl accompanies them as far as Mondoldo, the eighth island they visit. Here King Borabolla asks that Jarl be permitted to remain with him. Later word reaches the group that Jarl has been mysteriously murdered.

3. For Melville's relationship to Swift and Rabelais see Merrell R. Davis, *Melville's Mardi: A Chartless Voyage* (New Haven, 1952), pp. 142-59.

almost unanimous opinion of critics that Yillah is a symbol of perfection—ideal truth, goodness, and beauty.[4] She represents something that Taji has long sought: "For oh, Yillah; were you not the earthly semblance of that sweet vision, that haunted my earliest thoughts?" (I, 184). She had been set apart from humanity by the native priests, who reported her sayings as oracular whenever it suited their purposes. The killing of the priest Aleema frees Yillah from bondage to that sort of self-seeking power which needs the sanction of her authority. After she in turn eludes Taji, his quest for her is joined by statesman, historian, philosopher, and poet. Ultimately his companions, who find something approaching what they seek, if not Yillah, decide to discontinue the quest. Taji continues his chase alone, "over an endless sea" (II, 400), as the book ends.

Taji's search may be recognized as a quest for the authority of ultimate truth, the authority inherent in certainty, which together with the other ideals is part of the perfection Yillah represents. Although the actuality of place and event is soon left behind in this third work, *Mardi* continues and develops many ideas contained in *Typee* and *Omoo*. In the first two books one theme recurs: a general protest against authority. Melville next turns to an attempt to discover what type of authority can justifiably coerce man's obedience. Taji's quest in *Mardi* involves an examination of many kinds of authority and a rejection of all of them. Taji's search is a quest for ultimate truth, but the authoritative aspects of such truth, which bring man security and peace of mind, are stressed.

The spirit of Taji's quest validates Yillah as a symbol of authority. Often neither Taji nor his companions specifically mention Yillah in the visits to the many islands of Mardi. In the early narrative portion of the book, a spirit of adventure, continued from *Omoo*, prevails. The second half of *Mardi*

---

4. For a summary of the various interpretations see Tyrus Hillway, "Taji's Quest for Certainty," *American Literature*, XVIII (March, 1946), 30.

takes the reader into the world of the imagination, and, while the description of lore and geography drops to a minimum, symbolic description becomes more prominent. Emotional responses to ideas are substituted for the emotions arising from physical contact and experience. The shift marks an important change in Melville as a writer. His romantic reaction to exotic nature had been like Byron's response to the grandeur of Europe; now his technique resembles that of Carlyle. The frequency of metaphor, simile, and fantasy produces a different rhetoric, syntax, and grammar. The result is a seeming lack of precision in defining the quest. Within this rather vague outline the satire becomes like a cartoon, for only the more striking aspects of the countries visited are brought out. Melville is no longer describing a real world, and, with the exception of England which he had seen briefly on his Liverpool voyage, he had never visited the nations of Europe he is satirically representing. In *Mardi* the structural shift away from literalness reinforces the theme. The whole skeleton of the novel, a framework for the fantasy and caricature, reveals its meaning. Indeed, it is only by examining the narrative line of *Mardi*, which reveals the spirit of Taji's quest, that the mass of language falls away and permits the theme to emerge.

The authority of the ship captain, an important element of thematic concern in *Typee* and particularly in *Omoo,* is an element of minor concern at the beginning of *Mardi*. Again in the beginning of this third book Melville's sailor-narrator deserts his ship. This pattern of behavior has been repeated so often that the narrator in *Mardi* describes the whole affair with an almost apologetic attitude. The fact is that even with the best of captains Melville found the discipline of the sea extremely oppressive. The captain of the *Arcturion* is the fifth sea captain portrayed in the first three books. He is not mentioned by name, but he is a pleasant and benign master. Still the narrator complains impatiently about the voyage: "True, the skipper himself was a trump; stood upon no quarter-deck dignity; and he had a tongue for a sailor. Let me do him justice, furthermore . . . was sociable, nay loquacious, when I happened to stand at the helm. But what of that? Could he talk sentiment or philosophy? Not a bit" (I, 3). When placed beside Captain Vangs of the *Dolly,* Captain Guy of the *Julia,* or the French captain of the *Reine Blanche,* this captain is almost ideal. It is obvious that Melville's narrator does not expect him to be well versed in sentiment or philosophy. The narrator's other reason for jumping ship is equally invalid: the captain has abandoned his search for cachalot whales and is taking the ship far to the north to search for right whales near the Kamchatka Peninsula. The narrator contends that true whalemen take only cachalot, which is merely a rationalization, as Melville well knew. Actually the narrator is bored with the monotonous voyage and his dull companions and impatient with the many restrictions of shipboard life.

What happens aboard the *Arcturion* pictures the narrator as a rebel, one who is disinclined to submit to any authority. This same person will later tour the archipelago of Mardi as the white god Taji, and his refusal to accept the authority of the various Mardian institutions is in keeping with his character. Aboard the *Arcturion* he is quite provoked at the phlegmatic disposition of the crew, who remain content after three monotonous years of voyaging. The narrator who complained of the tyranny of his first skipper Captain Vangs, now would welcome a "spirited revolt" occasioned by some "despot of a captain" (I, 3). In view of the pattern of desertion, mutinous behavior, and revolt repeatedly occurring in the books, it begins to appear that Melville's narrator—and Melville himself because of his strong identification with his spokesmen—will refuse to be coerced by any authority for very long.

The elements conspire, however, to delay his departure from the *Arcturion,* because a calm overtakes the ship before he can steal a boat and escape. The stillness of the calm is bad for the morale of the seamen, but Melville's narrator dislikes the calm because "even his undoubted vested rights, comprised in his glorious liberty of volition, become as naught" (I, 10). To Melville the loss of his glorious liberty of volition, whether by a calm in the weather or the authority of the ship captain, is a positive affront. The picture of Melville's narrator, chafing under restraint aboard the *Arcturion* prior to deserting the ship, provides an insight into significant attitudes the narrator will hold as Taji in the second part of the book.

Taji's quest for Yillah throughout Mardi, a search for an authority to which he is intellectually willing to accord obedience, takes him to a variety of islands. The institutions he finds there, with one exception, are primarily political in nature. All purport to be authoritative. The island of Odo, ruled by King Media, is searched first. King Media is a rational and orthodox ruler; and under the guidance of this enlightened monarch Odo seems to be a happy land, but in secret places miserable serfs and war captives are held in bondage. There is also a party of democrats on Odo, "lean-visaged, poverty-stricken, and hence suspicious-looking varlets, grumbling and growling" (I, 214), that Media ruthlessly suppresses. Media's view is that the absolute monarch, ruling as a representative of an absolute God, can provide the greatest justice for his subjects. Here divine and political authority are equated in the traditional manner, and Taji shows at the same time the secret parts of Odo, "in whose inmost haunts . . . you heard most dismal cries, and voices cursing Media" (I, 224). Yillah is not found on Odo.

The next island visited is Valapee, where the failings of a democracy are satirized.[5] Valapee is ruled by King Peepi, a peculiar monarch because he has inherited all the souls of

5. My interpretation of the satire in Taji's visit to Valapee differs from that of Merrell Davis, who sees King Peepi only as a representative of foolish and wayward rulers without a conscience (pp. 155-56). "Valapee," however, suggests "Valley of the People," and "King Peepi" suggests "King of the People"—i.e., the ruler of a democracy. It seems reasonable that having pointed out the evils inherent in absolute monarchy in the first island visited, Melville would next turn to its opposite, democracy, in the second.

the island's dead heroes who preceded him. Not only has he inherited their souls, but he has also acquired their dominant personality traits. Thus his own personality is composed of "the headlong valour of the late Tongatona; the pusillanimous discretion of Blandoo; the cunning of Voyo; the simplicity of Raymonda; the prodigality of Zonoree, the thrift of Titonti" (I, 237). King Peepi is the most unreliable of rulers because "his assorted souls were uppermost and active in him, one by one" (I, 237). Subject to such impulses, the vacillating king is denuded of moral obligation to virtue, has no conscience, and by his very nature is unable to do right with any consistency. Here Melville is examining the institution of democratic government, as embodied in this king, and illustrating how the impulsive will of factions can push and pull national policy almost unchecked. None of the factions is held responsible for the lack of direction that results. Yillah is not found in Valapee.

The next Mardian island visited is Juam, where Taji meets a vice-ridden absolute monarch named Donjalolo. This king is characterized as having a "flexible elbow and a rigid spine" (I, 299). With all his drunkenness and tyranny, Donjalolo is not even constant to vice, but, forbidden by a higher law ever to leave his domain, he frequently lapses into reform in an effort to make his life more bearable, or at least different. Donjalolo fails to understand the higher law that he obeys, and Taji and his companions take this occasion to discuss the universal law, higher even than kings, and man's need to apprehend it. Taji remains skeptical about man's ability ever to perceive any such higher law. This skepticism is exhibited by Taji frequently as the group continues to pass by or visit several more islands that have various institutions lending themselves to satire: Quelquo, Nora-Bamma, Ohonoo, Tupia, Mondoldo, and Variora. On all these islands Yillah is not found.

In a lengthy section of the book in which Taji describes his visit to the island Maramma, Melville viciously attacks the authority of religious officialdom and the organized institution of the church. Maramma is ruled by the High Pontiff

Hivohitee, the "great lord paramount over many kings in Mardi" (II, 1). Since it is to Maramma that the majority of Mardians look for their religious dogma, what Melville writes about the authority of orthodox religion is concentrated primarily in this section. There are certain indications that the Roman Catholic Church is specifically under attack, as in the reference to Hivohitee MDCCCXLVIII (there had been a new pope in 1847), the description of the priests, and the selling of relics; but most of what Taji describes can be applied to any type of authoritarian religious orthodoxy. The first person Taji sees on the island is a blind priest and guide, Pani, who extracts exorbitant tolls from pilgrims who desire to tour the sacred island and climb the holy peak Ofo. Because of his blindness, Pani accepts the mysteries of the island on faith, but he speaks authoritatively about them. Pani is seen in contrast to one of the pilgrims Taji finds there, a young boy who wishes to climb Ofo by himself. The exchange between these two typifies the struggle between the authority of the church and the autonomy of the individual:

> "I go to ascend the peak," said the boy.
> "Then take me for a guide."
> "No, I am strong and lithesome. Alone must I go."
> "But how knowest thou the way?"
> "There are many ways; the right one I must seek for myself."
> "Ah, poor deluded one," sighed Pani; "but thus is it ever with youth; and rejecting the monitions of wisdom, suffer they must. Go on, and perish!"
> Turning, the boy exclaimed—"Though I act counter to thy counsels, oh Pani, I but follow the divine instinct in me" (II, 8-9).

But the religious hierarchy does more than merely express regret that the boy will not be guided. Pani is either dishonest or ignorant in this dialogue, because almost immediately afterward the boy is seized by other priests and carried away captive. They cannot permit their authority to be challenged. In the meantime Taji observes another incident that illustrates further Pani's untenable position. The blind guide points out the sacred stone image Doleema and calls it the flourishing holy tree Ananna. The location of these revered objects, standing near each other in a grove, apparently has been confused by Pani since he began his career as a guide. Later Taji observes Pani standing apart muttering to himself that he has doubts in his own "sightless soul" (II, 21) concerning what he tells the pilgrims. It would seem here that in Melville's view, reason, perhaps even intuition as well, is rather more necessary to religion than blind acceptance of authoritative church doctrine.

Taji also visits the idol-maker of the island, Hevaneva, who admits the idols he carves out of logs are actually logs until he receives his money for them, and then "they are as prime gods as ever were turned out in Maramma" (II, 38). The dread Hivohitee, who believes he has the power of life and death over all Mardians and temporal power over all the kings of Mardi, turns out to be merely "a bearded old hermit" living in a dark cell, "or at best, some equivocal conjuror" (II, 48). Taji rejects him as the supreme religious authority of Mardi with the same speed that he has rejected the officials on the island. As the group begins to leave Maramma, Babbalanja exclaims: "Yillah may have touched these shores; but long since she must have fled" (II, 30). Here is an indication that Melville believed that perhaps sometime in the past the authority of religious institutions may have been justified, but at present the church is characterized by a reliance on ritual and dogma that operates to the detriment of the true religious spirit.

The quest goes on through more of the Mardian islands where human failings continue to be viewed with a satiric spirit—Padulla, Pimminee, the Island of Fossils, Diranda, and Minda. Taji then turns to an exploration of certain Mardian islands that have identifiable counterparts in the real world. The first of these is Dominora (England), ruled by King Bello. This monarch is frantically engaged in a struggle to maintain the "Equipoise of Calabashes" (Balance of Power)

17

in his neighboring island Porpheero (Europe). The men of Dominora have been particularly noted as geographers, explorers, sailors, and empire-builders. Since they have the largest and best fleet of war canoes in Mardi, they believe the entire Mardian Lagoon belongs to them. Despite the fact that the whole island is a veritable garden, its system of class and privilege leaves many people starving. Taji and his party hear all about the adjacent island of Porpheero, with its collection of monarchs, each ruling a small kingdom. A brief caricature of each of the kings of Europe follows. The party starts out to land in Franko (France), but they are driven off by a violent volcanic eruption that takes place just as they approach.[6] They sail by Kaleedoni (Scotland) and Verdanna (Ireland), conversing about these islands as they pass. Then the voyagers turn to cross the wide waters to seek Yillah in the New Mardi, where "there or nowhere" (II, 210) they hope to find her.

After crossing the Mardian lagoon, the travelers hail the great island of Kolumbo (America) and pass by the portion of it called Kanneeda (Canada), which King Media predicts will soon be free from the mother country. When they arrive in Vivenza (United States), they begin their most extensive visit of the entire voyage. In Vivenza all men are free except the tribe of Hamo (Negroes). The party first arrives at the Great Central Temple (Senate) of Vivenza, which seems to them noisy, factious, and disorganized. Yet Taji finds freedom and prosperity in Vivenza. In his visit to South Vivenza he meets with "Nulli: a cadaverous, ghost-like man; with a low ridge of forehead; hair steel-gray; and wondrous eyes" (II, 248). With this Mardian counterpart of Calhoun he discusses the slavery of the Hamos, and the travelers apparently assent to the pronouncement of Babbalanja, who takes a moderate position on abolition: "Time, great philanthropist—Time must befriend these thralls!" (II, 252). If this expresses Melville's

6. Davis, p. 156, maintains that this eruption in Franko represents the revolution of 1848 and so dates the writing of this section of the book in the summer and fall of that year.

opinion on the matter, it is in marked contrast to the many spokesmen from New England who constantly preached abolition in strong terms.

The most serious indictment of the whole of Vivenza is against its chauvinistic attitude and its belief that the golden age is about to be established. According to Taji, the men of Vivenza, "having recently attained their national majority . . . were perhaps too much inclined to carry a vauntful crest" (II, 174). Vivenza is proud to have defeated Dominora, but Taji observes that the new nation was only defending its own shores. While the men of Vivenza taunt Dominora with charges of imperialism, they themselves are guilty of the same failing. Especially they "longed and lusted" to enjoy the "cluster of islets, green as new-fledged grass; and like the mouths of floating cornucopias" (II, 256), which lie to the south of Vivenza.

Furthermore, the men of Vivenza are admonished that, though they are free, their freedom arose from Vivenza's origins and geography, and that the state may not "forever remain liberal as now" (II, 241). This warning is voiced in a scroll read to a crowd in the northern section of Vivenza. Taji leaves "to the commentators on Mardi, some four or five hundred centuries hence" (II, 246) the identity of its anonymous author. The central message of the scroll is that freedom is not an end in itself. The scroll continues: ". . . freedom is more social than political. And its real felicity is not to be shared. *That* is of man's own individual getting and holding. It is not, who rules the state, but who rules me. Better be secure under one king, then exposed to the violence of twenty millions of monarchs, though oneself be of the number" (II, 244). Melville here adds a significant footnote to Taji's quest for authority by indicating that institutional authority may be less important than who rules the man, an individual and private problem. In the description of Vivenza Melville has given a realistic appraisal of the United States, its achievements and shortcomings. Taji fails to find Yillah here, but there is some optimism about America's future:

19

"She was promising as the morning," and in her "better aspect" a "noble land" (II, 175). To which Melville wryly adds: "Nevertheless, Vivenza was a braggadocio in Mardi" (II, 175).

There follows next a brief visit to Kolumbo of the South (South America), where live "bastard tribes and mongrel nations, wrangling and murdering to prove their freedom," and Media concludes that here "a tyrant would prove a blessing" (II, 258). Melville saw the dangers of anarchy and the need for some sort of political authority as a means to freedom. Then the travelers sail around the Cape of Capes and toward the Isles of the West. Yillah has not been found in New Mardi.

"The universe again before us; our quest, as wide"—the voyage goes on, Taji driven by the "blast resistless" (II, 275, 277). At this point, however, the locale of the search again changes. It is no longer an exploration of the islands of Mardi. Taji gazes over the sea and exclaims: "But this new world here sought, is stranger far than his, who stretched his vans from Palos. It is the world of mind" (II, 277). The remainder of the search is an exploration of the world of mind, of mythical isles that turn out to be equally as unsatisfying as the islands of Mardi. Even in that final island visited, Serenia, a sort of South Pacific Brook Farm, Taji does not find Yillah. His companions, who decide to remain in Serenia, urge him to abandon his quest: "Taji! for Yillah thou wilt hunt in vain; she is a phantom that but mocks thee" (II, 380). But Taji rejects Serenia because its people ignore the dark and violent aspects of human life, refusing to admit, for example, that there is a part of the world where there is not justice for all. He leaves the others in order to continue his search for the elusive Yillah.

Meville's narrator eloquently proclaims that he has full knowledge of what may be the result of his decision to press on: "So, if after all these fearful, fainting trances, the verdict be, the golden haven was not gained;—yet in bold quest thereof, better to sink in boundless deeps, than float on vulgar shoals; and give me, ye gods, an utter wreck, if wreck I do"

(II, 277). Here Taji speaks like an embryonic Captain Ahab, "a monomaniac in mad pursuit of an impossible goal."[7] The fatal pride is like Ahab's, but the difference is that Taji is still uncertain in his quest for an authoritative principle, while Ahab defied what he conceived to be the authority of God. For Taji determines to pursue his phantom though he be destroyed, but Captain Ahab hurls his harpoon with the certain knowledge of its inevitable result.

Melville's *Mardi*, with all its wide diversity of ideas, can well serve as a fictional representation of the intellectual physiognomy of America in the 1830's and 1840's. The many stirrings and doubts that assailed its philosophers and divines, the relentless scrutiny to which its institutions were subject, the underlying optimism that America was the hope of the world's peoples—all these are reflected in *Mardi*. Most of Melville's contemporaries, after probing and judging for themselves, stood ready to accept the authority of democratic institutions despite their defects, but the failure of Taji's quest indicates that a restless Melville was to continue searching. The decision was made with the full knowledge of the boundless deeps and the endless sea.

7. James E. Miller, Jr., "The Many Masks of *Mardi*," *Journal of English and Germanic Philology*, LVIII (1959), 412.

3. THE AUTHORITY
OF THE QUARTER-DECK

Melville's fictional account of his voyage to Liverpool in *Redburn* (1849) and his documentary novel of navy life in *White Jacket* (1850) have more in common than the fact that each book begins with its hero describing the unusual jacket that marks him off as a rather unique person. Both novels are initiation stories that "belong together in conception, spirit, and theme."[1] What was in the first novel an initial experience with seafaring life becomes in the second an initial experience with navy life. A major element in the initiation of each protagonist is his growing awareness of the coercing power of maritime authority—whether in the merchantman's less formal hierarchy of command or the complex institutionalized authority of the navy—and his response to it. The subtitle of *White Jacket*, "The World in a Man-of-War," points to another matter of thematic concern given emphasis in that book. White Jacket, less innocent of the world than Redburn as each begins his experience, is fully aware of the general human iniquity in this microcosmic world and of the need for an authority to govern. In both novels the captain is the central figure around whom the drama must inevitably be enacted.[2]

In the initiation of Wellingborough Redburn aboard the merchant ship *Highlander*, parental authority is completely destroyed. Redburn's father Walter Redburn had been a wealthy importer before his bankruptcy and subsequent

1. James E. Miller, Jr., "*Redburn* and *White Jacket*: Initiation and Baptism," *Nineteenth Century Fiction*, XIII (March, 1959), 273.
2. Power is always assumed as an adjunct to authority as these two books explore the anatomy of command. Melville's later "Benito Cereno" (1855) reveals the disorder attendant upon authority without power and the barbarity of power without authority. I have treated this elsewhere in "A New Reading of Melville's 'Benito Cereno,'" *Studies in American Literature* (Baton Rouge, 1960), pp. 49-57.

death, and the elder Redburn's highly romanticized accounts of travel and foreign lands had bred in his son a taste for the sea. The father's exotic stories hardly prove to be a sufficient guide for the young merchant seaman whose first duty aboard the *Highlander* is to clean a pigpen. At the end of the first chapter Melville symbolically tells the whole story. One of the prized possessions of Redburn's father had been an old-fashioned glass ship, which symbolizes for Redburn the romance of the sea and crystallizes his vague dream of travel into definite purpose. After a detailed description of the glass ship with its miniature fittings and occupants, Melville closes the chapter with Redburn's statement that the glass "figure-head, a gallant warrior in a cocked hat . . . fell from his perch the very day I left home to go to sea" (9). In retrospect Redburn realizes that his romantic notions of seafaring life were based upon rather fragile substance. As the years pass, parts of the glass ship break and shatter, and it is no coincidence that the disintegration begins on the day that Redburn set off to sea.

Still another authority destroyed in *Redburn*—a kind of extension of the authority of parents—is that of guidebooks and, ultimately, all literature. Walter Redburn had not only reported his experiences to his son, but he had also left him a collection of books about foreign lands. One of these books was a guidebook to Liverpool entitled *A Picture of Liverpool*. The grand hotels, pleasant concourses, majestic buildings, and beautiful vistas shown in this guidebook bear little resemblance to the Liverpool Redburn encounters. Redburn's Liverpool consists of a disreputable sailors' boardinghouse, dingy taverns, vice dens, and a poverty-stricken and disease-ridden populace. In sadness Redburn reflects that "this precious book was next to useless" because "the thing that had guided the father could not guide the son" (200). Starting with this proposition, Redburn then generalizes that "all literature, in one sense, is made up of guide-books" (201), and yet each age must make its own guidebook because older ones are not reliable. Through Redburn's new awareness

Melville implies here that while recorded experience in literature constitutes an authority that can coerce belief, whatever is believed may be irrelevant or invalid when applied to present experience.

The initiation of a gentleman's son into the society of a merchantman's crew provides the context in which the grand authority of the captain himself will be seen to function. Redburn finds that seafaring life has new rules to match his new circumstances. He is forced to conform to the mores of a new society, although he never actually becomes a part of it. He quickly discovers the ship's hierarchy of command; he learns that he owes instant obedience to the two mates. An early lesson in the discipline of the sea occurs when he is told to gather up some carpenter's shavings and put them in a particular place. He makes the mistake of collecting the trash into what he selects as a better place and then protesting to the mate when he is rudely ordered to correct his error. When the mate flies into a terrible rage, storms at his new sailor, and repeats the order without explanation, Redburn comments: "This was my first lesson in the discipline of the sea, and I never forgot it. From that time I learned that sea-officers never gave reasons for anything they order to be done. It is enough that they command it" (36). The other members of the crew as well as the officers force Redburn to conform. He learns the many unwritten rules governing behavior while living, sleeping, and eating in the limited quarters of the ship allotted to the sailors, and the rules are enforced by the sailors themselves. Redburn is taunted about his genteel background and told to stay out of the way of his betters or face the prospect of being pitched overboard. He is extremely unhappy with his new companions: "I loathed, detested, and hated them . . . and I thought myself the most forlorn and miserable wretch that ever breathed" (65-66). He makes the outward voyage without a single friend or companion among the crew, and he becomes, in his words, "a sort of Ishmael in the ship" (79).

The absolute authority of the ship captain makes the greatest impression on the greenhorn sailor. Captain Riga of the *Highlander* is scarcely ever seen aboard the ship by the lowly sailor Redburn, but the captain's presence is felt by all aboard. Redburn does not understand why it is necessary for the captain to remain aloof from his crew, and, indeed, Redburn at one time contemplates a social call on the ship's master in his quarters. This idea is rudely jeered by the sailors, and only the intervention of the chief mate prevents the completion of Redburn's expedition. Even Redburn's attempt to strike up a casual conversation with the captain on the deck is rebuffed, and Redburn fails to understand what he believes to be Captain Riga's change in attitude toward him. The captain had seemed very cordial, Redburn remembers, when he had signed the ship's articles while the *Highlander* was still riding in New York harbor. Gradually Redburn becomes aware of the position the captain holds while at sea and the authority he wields, but Redburn in his own mind puts Captain Riga down as a sort of imposter, "for no gentleman would have treated another gentleman as he did me" (91). On the homeward voyage Redburn finds that even the ship's passengers, emigrants from Europe bound for New York, are subject to Captain Riga's absolute authority: "For the emigrants in these ships are under a sort of martial law; and in all their affairs are regulated by the despotic ordinances of the captain. And though it is evident that to a certain extent this is necessary, and even indispensable; yet, as at sea no appeal lies beyond the captain, he too often makes unscrupulous use of his power. And as for going to law with him at the end of the voyage, you might as well go to law with the Czar of Russia" (340). Early in his experience at sea Redburn has learned that unscrupulous captains may use their authority merely to further their own tyrannical power. Captain Riga is no better nor worse than most sea captains, but his rule seems despotic to Redburn. While he notes that the authority of the ship captain is legally constituted, he also observes the practical difficulty of attempting to hold the captain responsible to the law for his actions.

These are among the lessons of the sea that Melville-Redburn learned early in his seafaring career.

Redburn's account of his return voyage to New York is brief and mainly concerned with the shipboard experiences of a new friend acquired in England who returns with him. Harry Bolton, a profligate young aristocrat who has spent his inheritance on gambling, meets Redburn in Liverpool, where Harry has found himself without funds. He decides to ship off to America aboard the *Highlander* to recover his fortunes. Harry Bolton's initiation into the discipline of the sea on the return voyage provides an implicit comment on Redburn's earlier experiences on the first crossing. The young men are much alike, but the rigidly inflexible Harry dresses as a dandy and will not perform the tasks assigned him. His life is made extremely miserable, demonstrating the worst that could have happened to Redburn had he been less adaptable.[3] Because Redburn was able to obey the authority of the crew and captain, he did not, as Harry does, "become a hunted hare to the merciless crew" (333). Yet when he speaks at length of Harry's plight, Redburn is obviously speaking also of his own initiation: "Few landsmen can imagine the depressing and self-humiliating effect of finding one's self, for the first time, at the beck of illiterate sea-tyrants, with no opportunity of exhibiting any trait about you, but your ignorance of everything connected with the sea-life that you lead, and the duties you are constantly called on to perform" (333). Ultimately Redburn leaves Harry in New York, and his English friend signs aboard a whaling ship bound for the Pacific. Years later Redburn learns that Harry has met his death by falling overboard in a far-off ocean and being crushed by a whale at the side of the ship. The ship, a Nantucket whaler, is appropriately named the *Huntress*.

In *White Jacket* (1850) Melville presents an extensive

---

3. H. Bruce Franklin, "Redburn's Wicked End," *Nineteenth Century Fiction*, XX (September, 1965), 190-94, which explores the significance of Harry Bolton as Redburn's double, provides a good summary of the criticism on the Redburn-Bolton relationship.

documentation of the United States Navy version of the discipline of the sea. Drawing upon his own experiences once again, Melville chronicles his homeward voyage from Honolulu beginning in August, 1843, aboard the navy frigate *United States*. The narrator of the novel, nicknamed White Jacket by the crew because of the handmade white duck frock he habitually wears, describes the cruise of the warship *Neversink* from the Pacific around Cape Horn to Norfolk harbor. Although the *Neversink*, commanded by Captain Claret and carrying a commodore as supernumerary, touches on the coast of Peru and at Rio de Janiero during the course of the voyage, incidents ashore are not included in the narrative. *White Jacket* is a detailed account of life aboard a United States warship in the mid-nineteenth century, a picture of what Melville calls in the subtitle of the book "The World in a Man-of-War."

In *White Jacket* the concentration on the microcosmic man-of-war and the limited locale that necessarily results gives the theme of the authority of the captain and the discipline of the sea a great intensity. Melville portrays a variety of professional ship captains in his books dealing with the sea, but none other with the fullness of detail that delineates Captain Claret. The captain's exercise of authority strikes a kind of average among Melville's fictional captains. He is not as tyrannical as Captain Vangs of the *Dolly* or Captain Riga of the *Highlander,* nor is he weak and ineffectual like Captain Guy of the *Julia*. The ships' masters who appear in the earlier books tend to illustrate some limited aspect of a captain's authority. In Captain Claret of the *Neversink* Melville thoroughly explores the anatomy of command.

The highest ranking officer aboard the *Neversink* is the unnamed commodore, but he holds himself so far aloof from the daily routine of the cruise that he seldom appears in the narrative. The commodore's words are directed only to the captain, and he seldom interferes in the government of the ship. On several occasions the commodore's presence does add to the ceremonial duties of the sailors as he is rowed about in his barge to visit other ships or call at foreign ports. Since there are so few times when sailors come in contact with the commodore, White Jacket asserts that it may be thought that "since he so seldom appears on the stage, he cannot be so august a personage after all" (358-59). But Melville's narrator avers that actually the reverse is true, since "the mightiest potentates keep the most behind the veil" (359). Because the commodore is so far removed from the routine duties of the crew, it is Captain Claret who represents to them the chief force of authority.

Captain Claret of the *Neversink* is neither better nor worse than most ship captains in assuming and exercising his command and in meeting all the responsibilities his position entails. Although Captain Claret is guilty of certain acts that appear to White Jacket as unnecessarily cruel, he is not pictured as fundamentally a bad man. A point made repeatedly by the narrator is that whatever Captain Claret is, "the usages of the Navy had made him" (463), and so it is clear that the protests are directed against the abuses inherent in the system, not merely against one of its products who happens to be in command on this ship. The captain's authority is based upon law, and the law makes his authority absolute: "It is no limited monarchy, where the sturdy Commons have a right to petition, and snarl if they please; but almost a despotism, like the Grand Turk's. The captain's word is law; he never speaks but in the imperative mood. When he stands on his quarter-deck at sea, he absolutely commands as far as eye can reach" (27). And the captain has the needed power to enforce his commands. He alone controls the disposition of the small arms aboard the ship, and he and his officers wear swords at their sides ready for instant use. The police force of the ship—the master-at-arms with his ship's corporals and marines carrying rattan sticks—is under the captain's direct command. Authority cannot function properly without this power, and no power aboard the ship other than the captain's is authorized.

During the course of the voyage White Jacket occasionally

describes Captain Claret in a favorable light. Many of his actions make for the higher morale and greater welfare of the five hundred men entrusted to his charge. In the matter of provisions for his crew, for example, Captain Claret is particularly conscientious. He sees that the appropriate officers maintain the ship's stores in good condition, make drinking water available in plentiful supply, and distribute rations equitably to the crew. When the ship is in port, local traders with the captain's permission bring fresh fruit to the sailors, who are glad to purchase it to relieve the monotony of their diet. White Jacket comments on the lift given to morale by this policy. Captain Claret also sees that the sick are promptly cared for aboard the ship, or at least that they are relieved from duty and turned over to Surgeon Cuticle. Their treatment at his hands is not always beneficial, but the captain rigidly enforces the navy rule that seamen who are genuinely ill cannot be forced to work or attend muster.

As a disciplinarian, on some occasions, Captain Claret shows humanity. His treatment of the young midshipmen aboard the *Neversink,* who are the bane of the sailors, particularly appeals to Melville's sailor-narrator. The ship carries a full complement of these youths training to be officers. Since as far as sailors are concerned they have the status of officers, and because their age often makes their commands capricious and irresponsible, they are thoroughly disliked by the crew. When Captain Claret acts to put these young boys in their place, he is in effect showing sympathy for his persecuted sailors. Although the captain can legally punish the midshipmen only by suspending them from duty, he finds other means to control their boisterous conduct. His favorite method is to order them to stand in the rigging until he says that they can come down. On one occasion when a midshipman is insubordinate to him, he orders the quartermaster to pitch overboard the culprit's hammock and personal belongings. The sailors, of course, view this kind of discipline with silent glee.

Unfortunately, when the sailors quarrel with the midshipmen, the years and experience of the sailors are not judged to be of equal importance with the boys' official rank in the hierarchy of authority. While Captain Claret may quickly put down any challenge to his own authority by these young men, he takes the part of the midshipmen over the sailors no matter how ridiculous the midshipmen's demands may be. White Jacket protests that "however childish, ignorant, stupid, or idiotic a midshipman, if he but orders a sailor to perform even the most absurd action, that man is not only bound to render instant and unanswering obedience, but he would refuse at his peril" (270). The fault, as White Jacket sees it, is in the system that places these young tyrants on board a man-of-war.

Captain Claret also has the perspicacity to remit his harsh discipline toward the crew in other instances when the circumstances warrant it. Once when a belaying pin thrown in the dark comes perilously close to his ear, he chooses to ignore it, although he could have ordered mass punishment. When White Jacket is reported to the captain by the mate because he had not been at his proper post during the tacking of the ship, a maneuver with which he was not familiar, the captain at first orders the narrator to the gangway to be flogged. When it is demonstrated, however, that White Jacket did not know where his post was, the captain orders him released. Captain Claret makes it a policy to ignore curses directed at him and his officers by men who have just been released from being flogged at the gangway. He knows that the dire threats common at such moments are to be expected and not heard. In the same fashion he is lenient with men who have just returned from liberty ashore when these men, invariably in an advanced state of intoxication, make insulting remarks to the officers as they step aboard. Since it is Captain Claret's policy to ignore the drunken sallies of wit and abuse forthcoming on such occasions, the sailors take full advantage of the temporary leniency, often shouting abusive remarks about the officers or the captain while feigning intoxication.

30

While Melville portrays Captain Claret as having a certain flexibility in his command of the warship, which is of course part of the strategy of a good captain, more frequently Claret is cruel and inhuman in his absolute rule. There are several personal traits evinced by the captain that, when magnified by his position of absolute authority, cause his discipline to be either more severe or less impartial than necessary. He is a heavy drinker. The sailors often notice in their captain a "peculiarly lustreless . . . eye," an "unnecessarily methodical step," and the "forced firmness of his whole demeanour" (139). Of course, an impersonal, methodical, and firm bearing on the part of a captain may tend to strengthen his authority, but these signs in the case of Captain Claret result from the fact that he "continually kept himself in an uncertain equilibrio between soberness and its reverse" (139). In short, Claret is a characterizing name. Once his imbibing nearly proves disastrous in the emergency of a storm, and White Jacket believes it to be the source of his unreasonable attitude toward the sailors on other occasions.

Captain Claret is also a man who can harbor a grudge. This personal characteristic causes a foretopman by the name of Candy to get a flogging. After noticing Candy making gestures which he takes to be mocking him, the captain two days later singles Candy out from among a group of sailors not hoisting a sail fast enough and orders him flogged. White Jacket also dislikes the captain's habit of condescending to play the jolly fellow with the men during the periods of recreation on deck, because Captain Claret seems to return to an even greater severity immediately afterwards. Melville's narrator bitterly asserts that "of all insults, the temporary condescension of a master to a slave is the most outrageous and galling" (347). White Jacket further warns: "That potentate who most condescends, mark him well; for that potentate, if occasion come, will prove your uttermost tyrant" (347). Finally, the captain is inclined to accept unobtrusive bribes at times. All the crew notice that when Bland, the master-at-arms, is caught in the act of smuggling, his pun-

31

ishment is tempered by the fact that the captain has received gifts from him of a rare snuff box made from a whale's tooth and a gold mounted Brazilian cane. These items had been part of Bland's purchases ashore to be smuggled aboard, together with his usual contraband liquor. White Jacket points out that the captain should have felt obligated "to decline all presents from his subordinates" so that "the sense of gratitude would not have operated to the prejudice of justice" (235).

Whether Captain Claret happens to be at a given moment a competent commander or a harsh and unfeeling martinet, certainly his responsibility as a captain is much more important than good or bad personal traits. Everything that happens during the voyage stems from his authority as a ship's master, and whatever is done in the name of discipline, whatever minor tyrants exist with his permission among the ship's officers, whatever human rights are abrogated by the marine police force—all these occur under the captain's direct jurisdiction. The captain is responsible for his subordinates as well as for himself, and all exercising of authority aboard the vessel that he commands is a matter of his concern. The discipline aboard a man-of-war, as set down by law and reinforced by years of seafaring tradition, theoretically is the same on any naval vessel, but in practice it takes its character on any specific ship from the severity with which a captain exercises his own authority. Aboard the *Neversink* the discipline in general is oppressive and tyrannical.

Although the whole of *White Jacket* may be construed as a protest against the harshness, inhumanity, and cruelty that Melville had observed in his own navy career, he recognized the need, nevertheless, for some kind of effective discipline to control the large crew of a warship and to direct its operation efficiently. Early in the book, Melville's narrator, when discussing the ship's strict rules, remarks that "were it not for these regulations, a man-of-war's crew would be nothing but a mob" (7). It will never be possible aboard a warship to avoid tyranny completely. White Jacket draws this conclusion in logical fashion: the purpose of a man-of-war is to fight battles with an enemy, and during a war certain individual rights must be ignored for the good of the entire fighting force. While the discipline aboard the *Neversink* is considered by White Jacket a necessary evil, he believes the administration of it could be accomplished with much more fairness and justice.

The kind of sailor that the oppressive and tyrannical officers of the *Neversink* profess to admire, according to White Jacket, is "a fellow without shame, without a soul, so dead to the least dignity of manhood that he could hardly be called a man" (485). It is interesting to read his description of this ideal sailor (from the point of view of the officers) while keeping in mind the character of Melville's spokesmen in all his novels dealing with the sea and recalling the frequency with which they become involved in desertion, mutinous behavior, and rebellion against authority. White Jacket protests: "Whereas, a seaman who exhibits traits of moral sensitiveness, whose demeanour shows dignity within; this is the man they, in many cases, instinctively dislike. The reason is, they feel such a man to be a continual reproach to them, as being mentally superior to their power. He has no business in a man-of-war; they do not want such men. To them there is insolence in his manly freedom, contempt in his very carriage" (485-86). White Jacket is here describing some seamen like his much admired friend Jack Chase and, undoubtedly, himself. The passage may well serve as a summary of Melville's own general reaction to the discipline of the sea. It gives the reader a picture of the sensitive, dignified, mentally superior, freedom-loving Melville thrust in among the unregenerate crew of a man-of-war, where, in truth, he had no business.

White Jacket also contains a vigorous protest against the whole system of authority that governs the navy—a ringing denunciation of the cruelties perpetrated by those serving the system, a condemnation of the evils inherent in the system itself, and a rejection of the laws that sanction the

33

system's existence. The protest against the cruelty and inhumanity of those in authority aboard the *Neversink* takes specific form in White Jacket's description of several floggings that occur during the voyage and his denunciation of this barbaric practice. When the call is sounded throughout the ship for all hands to assemble to witness punishment, White Jacket avers that the "summons sounds like a doom," and he approaches the scene with a "sense of degradation, pity, and shame" (167). The practice is hated because of the pain it inflicts and because it is a reminder of the oppression under which they all live. What makes the cruelty even worse, according to White Jacket, is that the men who are flogged are not even criminals in the accepted sense of the word, but have merely violated "arbitrary laws" (172). In theory only the captain or a court martial is empowered by law to order corporal punishment, and it must be administered at the gangway with the surgeon in attendance. In practice, however, the boatswain's mates carry a "colt" or rope's end curled in their hats and use it on the sailors' backs the moment the captain directs them to do so. The law limits to twelve the number of lashes with the cat-o-nine-tails a captain can order inflicted at any one time. A court-martial can direct more severe punishment, but captains often subvert the law by ordering several series of lashings with brief intervals in between. The most barbarous flogging practice of all, known as "flogging through the fleet," is witnessed only once by White Jacket during the cruise. Since a court-martial is empowered by the Articles of War to sentence a culprit to a flogging not to exceed one hundred lashes per offense, and since often the sentence is increased by construing one act as a violation of several articles, a seaman can be literally flogged to death within the limits of the law. When such a sentence is adjudged, the culprit may be ordered "flogged through the fleet" as an object lesson to his fellow sailors. The prisoner is rowed through the squadron of warships to receive a portion of his sentence at each ship, with a fresh boatswain's mate wielding the cat at each gangway.

34

White Jacket centers his protest on the abrogation of the sailors' rights as citizens while they are serving at sea. Not only do the captains violate the law when they order protracted floggings, but they also violate constitutional rights by keeping sailors indefinitely imprisoned in the brig, sometimes upon only the most unsubstantial allegation of misconduct. White Jacket cites an example of such abuse when Captain Claret confines a sailor "for upward of a month" because of "motives of personal pique" (179). The narrator believes that seamen should have the same guarantees of law other citizens have, and he points out how the whole system of authority aboard a man-of-war violates the Constitution. Congress, by virtue of the enactment of the naval code, has authorized captains to violate the spirit of constitutional guarantees, especially in the provisions that offenses not specifically dealt with in the Articles of War "be punished according to the laws and customs in such cases at sea" (178). Captains use this terminology to justify such punishments as "flogging through the fleet." Still worse, customs dictate different treatment for officers and sailors. An officer can only be punished by court-martial, and this procedure is rarely invoked except for the most serious breach of regulations. The punishment of flogging is especially a violation of rights because it is not universally applied. Since these laws governing seamen are immoral, White Jacket believes sailors "would be morally justified in resisting . . . to the uttermost; and, in so resisting, would be religiously justified in what would be judicially styled 'the act of mutiny' itself" (181). This statement by White Jacket, justifying mutiny by the sailors as a means of securing their rights, is his most violent and incendiary protest in the entire book.

White Jacket, therefore, scornfully attacks the Articles of War, the laws that sanction the system of discipline aboard a warship. He says, however, that he holds "no sentimental and theoretic love for the common sailor; no romantic belief in that peculiar noble-heartedness and exaggerated generosity of disposition fictitiously imputed to him in novels; and no

prevailing desire to gain the reputation of being his friend"
(381). The world aboard a man-of-war is a world rife with
evil; it must be governed by an authority. Yet the sailors'
iniquities are encouraged and increased by the "morally de-
basing effects of the unjust, despotic, and degrading laws
under which the man-of-war's man lives" (382). Therefore
at many points in the novel White Jacket suspends the narrative in order to call directly upon the reader to bring pres-
sure on the Congress to modify the Articles of War. These
laws, clothing the captain in his absolute authority and sanc-
tioning the oppressive discipline of the sea, are ultimately to
blame for most of the injustice in the world of the man-of-
war.

The youthful sailor who in *Redburn* was slightly bewildered
and then embittered by the harsh ways of seafaring life
becomes the knowledgeable White Jacket by the end of the
navy experience. Since Redburn's old world was so thoroughly
shattered and his new one so full of confusing new experiences, his book must be less intensely focused. White Jacket
naturally has a further initiation to undergo because the warship differs from the merchantman, but an equal emphasis is
given in his book to a thoughtful analysis of the anatomy of
command and a documentation of the abuses that spring
from a misuse of the authority of the quarter-deck.

4. AHAB AND THE
AUTHORITY OF GOD

Ishmael's introduction of himself to the reader in the first
lines of *Moby-Dick* (1851) invites careful attention to his
name and history, and yet the first brief chapter in this book,
which supplies the context for the entire subsequent action,
has been largely overlooked by critics seeking to formulate a
theme for Melville's greatest work. Certainly a major theme
of *Moby-Dick* is implicit in this opening chapter, which Melville entitled "Loomings."[1] The theme implied in the first
chapter is admittedly obscure in its outlines, but Ishmael's
characterization of himself and his discussion of his reasons
for going to sea reward the most careful attention. Melville's
identification with each of the narrators of his novels told in
the first person is manifestly obvious. The young Redburn,
whose romantic notions took him to sea; Tommo, the rover
in Polynesia; Taji, the voyager in the world of the mind;
White Jacket, who chafed under the harsh authority of naval
discipline—these are not four separate characters. They are
one consistent character with four names. Now in *Moby-Dick*
a fifth name is added, as Melville invites the reader to call
him Ishmael.

Melville put much of the theme of this book before the
reader in the name of the narrator. It will be remembered
that in the Biblical story God gave to Abraham and his
bondswoman Hagar a son to be called by that name, and the
Lord commanded: "And he will be a wild man; his hand will
be against every man, and every man's hand against him."[2]
It was thus determined before Ishmael was born that he

---

1. A looming, by dictionary definition, is an indistinct form usually
large or threatening, coming into sight, especially over the surface of the
sea. A second meaning of the word anticipates the loom image—the inter-
weaving of fate, free will, and chance—in Chapters XLVII ("The Mat-
Maker") and CII ("A Bower in the Arsacides").

2. Gen. 16:12.

should be a rover and by his nature oppose the coercing restrictions of authority. Later in the Biblical story Ishmael was cast out with Hagar to wander in the wilderness because he mocked his half-brother Isaac. Yet this casting out of Ishmael had been clearly predetermined, and Ishmael was made what he was because it was God's will. Two ideas, therefore, are implicit in the story of Ishmael, and both of them are applicable to *Moby-Dick*. The first concerns Ishmael the wanderer, the wild man whose hand is against every man's; the second, Ishmael the subject of God's inscrutable authority.

The Ishmael of *Moby-Dick* is also a rover who has little or no money in his purse and nothing particular to interest him ashore. Yet the sea has a strange attraction for him: "Whenever I find myself growing grim about the mouth; whenever it is a damp, drizzly November in my soul; whenever I find myself involuntarily pausing before coffin warehouses, and bringing up the rear of every funeral I meet; and especially whenever my hypos get such an upper hand of me, that it requires a strong moral principle to prevent me from deliberately stepping into the street, and methodically knocking people's hats off—then, I account it high time to get to sea as soon as I can. This is my substitute for pistol and ball. With a philosophical flourish Cato throws himself on his sword; I quietly take to the ship" (1). The anti-authoritarian Ishmael is subject to a melancholy brought about primarily because he lacks a strong moral principle. This principle is the authority (in other guises, in earlier books) that he has searched for but never found. He has discovered, however, that a good substitute for it—though admittedly only a substitute, still better than pistol and ball—is to place himself under the authority of a ship captain. In this way his external life is well ordered by a strong authority, which, paradoxically, gives freer reign to that internal and more spiritual existence. Though Ishmael recognizes that his solution is a drastic one when he compares the gravity and finality of it to suicide, the discipline of the sea need not be absolutely final if all goes well, and in the meantime he finds its effects salutary. Ishmael's second reason for going to sea is contained in a lengthy, lyrical passage on man's love for the mysteries of the ocean— as expressed by mythologist, historian, and poet—and the chance for speculation the deep sea affords, because "meditation and water are wedded for ever" (2). In summary, Ishmael says for him the sea is "the image of the ungraspable phantom of life; and this is the key to it all" (3). Next Ishmael voices his concern with "the grand programme of Providence that was drawn up a long time ago" (5) as opposed to his "own unbiased freewill and discriminating judgment" (6) as determining factors in his decision to go to sea. This complex problem raises the question of divine authority in his own life, which constitutes the ultimate mystery. Thus the narrator establishes his kinship with his Biblical namesake.

Ishmael, then, in the hope of discovering the key to ultimate questions, yields for the moment his independence and freedom of social action—where such yielding is normal and even essential—aboard a ship. By placing himself under the external discipline of a ship's master, Ishmael will be able to free his immediate person from the vagaries of aimless wandering and to devote his inner energies to the larger, cosmic problems of fate, free will, and chance. The first chapter ends with a reference to "one grand hooded phantom, like a snow hill in the air" (6), which is, of course, the vague, looming outline of Moby Dick. Thus the symbolic white whale is alluded to even before Ishmael leaves New York and travels to Nantucket where he will join the *Pequod* to sail under Captain Ahab. It is important to note the occurrence of this image here, because here and throughout the novel the white whale is for Ishmael a symbol of inscrutability, while for Ahab it represents divine malice, enhanced of course by mystery. The distinction is vital to an understanding of Melville's theme.

After the first chapter of *Moby-Dick* the thematic relationships and variations become quite complex. Determined to

seek the authority of a whaling ship's discipline and drawn
to the sea by the mysteries that lurk in its depths, Ishmael
places himself under the command of Captain Ahab, whose
authority reflects a strong immoral principle rather than a
moral one. At least it is a strong principle. Again in *Moby-
Dick* the environment of the sea, which requires that such
absolute authority be invested in one man, provides a setting
in which Captain Ahab's absolutism (up to a point) is a
necessity. But there is a unique and grave seriousness to
Captain Ahab's position as a ship's master, because Ahab
tyrannically coerces not only the bodies but also the souls of
his crew. So powerful is the sway that Ahab achieves over
his men that it enables him even to engender their enthusiasm
for the diabolical pursuit of Moby Dick, which is not only
spiritually dangerous, but—what is perhaps more important
to these workers in the sperm oil industry—unprofitable as
well.

Before Captain Ahab appears in the narrative there are
signs that Ishmael will feel a certain sympathy for his commander. Ishmael's first view of the *Pequod,* for example,
provokes the comment: "A noble craft, but somehow a most
melancholy!" (69). Ishmael will find Ahab himself possessed
abundantly of the qualities of nobility and melancholy. Ishmael has occasion to remark about Ahab that "all men tragi-
cally great are made so through a certain morbidness" (73).
As demonstrated in the opening chapter of the book, Ishmael
himself is often morbid and melancholy, and so he, more than
any other man aboard the *Pequod,* will sympathize with this
captain in whom he recognizes greatness. Yet their purposes
are not the same. Captain Ahab enters the narrative as the
sultan of the *Pequod,* to whose absolute authority Ishmael
has subjected himself for the duration of the voyage. Captain
Ahab has already encountered the white whale; he believes
he has been maliciously scarred. Now he is determined to
avenge himself. Ishmael will learn of all this, and his similar
cast of mind and spirit will prompt his sympathy for Ahab.
This sympathy explains in part the sway Ahab exercises over

Ishmael as he too is carried along in the vengeful hunt for Moby Dick.

Ahab's authority is evil; Ishmael indicates that Ahab is aware of his Satanic quality. In a moment of introspection just before the *Pequod* encounters Moby Dick, Captain Ahab, ruminating on thoughts of death and immortality, calls a halt to his meditations by exclaiming: "So far gone am I in the dark side of earth, that its other side, the theoretic bright one, seems but uncertain twilight to me" (520-21). The passage is reminiscent of John's warning in the gospel: "And this is the condemnation, that light has come into the world, and men loved darkness rather than light, because their deeds were evil."[3] There is a symbolic correspondence between Ahab and the "prince of darkness" as opposed to the God of light. Ahab's dominion begins with his authority as a ship captain, because law and seafaring tradition establish him as the supreme ruler of his ship, but he successfully extends his sway even beyond that. Commanding a pagan ship manned almost entirely by a pagan crew, he reveals his diabolism to Ishmael and especially to Starbuck, the chief mate. The very moment Ahab first steps to the *Pequod*'s quarter-deck, Ishmael notes his "nameless regal overbearing dignity" (122). Here is a captain endowed not only with the requisite dignity of his office, but possessed as well with an eminence that must remain nameless because it is outside of man's normal experience. Captain Ahab is frequently referred to by various members of the crew as "the Old Mogul," an obvious reference to the oriental absoluteness of his authority. The epithet reveals the crew's recognition of a type of sway not usually associated with ship captains because it connotes a cruel indifference to the welfare of his subordinates aboard the ship.

Once the purpose of the *Pequod*'s voyage becomes apparent to the sailors, Captain Ahab needs all the skill he can command in order to enlist their active participation in his personal vendetta. He is equal to this task. Realizing that finan-

3. John 3:19.

cial reward is a strong motive, Ahab calls the crew together and nails a Spanish gold doubloon to the mast, offering it to the first sailor who raises Moby Dick. He then gathers his harpooners around him and, pouring liquor into the hollow of their harpoons, orders them to drink and swear death to Moby Dick. The ceremony is designed to help Ahab control his sailors in the long pursuit that will follow. When the crew members later return to the normal expectations connected with a whaling voyage, they sense the evil they have done at their captain's instigation, and in their minds the hunt for Moby Dick becomes invested with a "strange imaginative impiousness" (210). Hearing certain fearful rumblings among the crew, Ahab distracts their attention by setting them to the ordinary routine task of killing whales. He realizes that by having disclosed somewhat prematurely the real purpose of the voyage, "he had indirectly laid himself open to the un-answerable charge of usurpation; and with perfect impunity, both moral and legal, his crew if so disposed . . . could re-fuse all further obedience to him, and even violently wrest from him the command" (211). Shrewdly Ahab diverts them by keeping them busy with a few whales, and thus he prevents just such an eventuality. Later when lightning strikes the ship in a storm, the sailors become so panic-stricken that Ahab finds it necessary to recall their oaths to them in order to maintain their cooperation in continuing the hunt. After the white whale is sighted, Ahab promises much more gold to the crew, and on the third day of the desperate conflict with Moby Dick he can maintain his authority only by threatening to fling a harpoon through any man who jumps in terror out of the whaleboat. Thus by relying alternately on promises of reward and threats of violence, Ahab retains control of the crew on the dangerous and evil mission. While his methods include getting his men emotionally involved in the hunt, demanding oaths from them, bribing them, and even resorting to violence if necessary, Captain Ahab also knows when to divert their attention from the pursuit to other matters of commonplace nature. The flexibility and imagination of Ahab's methods of command demonstrate his skill in maintaining his authority over his crew.

Captain Ahab's purpose in creating a sphere in which he has absolute sway is to challenge the authority of God. Even before Ishmael meets the captain of the *Pequod*, he receives hints of this purpose. The significance of the prophetic warnings of Elijah, whose Biblical counterpart prophesied the disobedience of King Ahab, is not lost on Ishmael as he leaves the ship after signing for the voyage. Captain Peleg, one of the owners of the ship, answers Ishmael's inquiry about the absent Ahab with the remark: "He's a grand, ungodly, god-like man, Captain Ahab" (79). Ahab is ungodly because he is evil, Satanic; he cannot accept the authority of God, and in ruling over his own domain aboard ship he becomes god-like. Because Ahab's domain is extra-Christian, the Captain surrounds himself with pagan henchmen. The American Indian tribe from which the *Pequod* derives its name exists outside of Christendom. Ishmael finds that the three harpooners aboard the *Pequod* are pagans who serve Ahab's purpose admirably: the Polynesian Queequeg, the wild American Indian Tashtego, and the giant Negro savage Daggoo. The three mates of the *Pequod* present varying attitudes toward whaling and toward Ahab's quest. The chief mate Starbuck is a religious man who might be called the conscience of the *Pequod*, and as such he does not fit directly Ahab's plans. Yet Ahab successfully manipulates him for his own purposes, often relying on Starbuck's "Christian" responses with a kind of diabolic genius. Stubb, the second mate, is an indifferent, fearless fatalist; Flask, the materialistic third mate, is the most pugnacious and determined killer of whales aboard the ship. Stubb and Flask are both quite ready to follow Ahab wherever he leads them.

Captain Ahab, however, is not satisfied to rely on the normal complement of sailors aboard the *Pequod* for the hunting of Moby Dick, and therefore he smuggles five extra men aboard to form his own boat crew. They are soon revealed to the sailors as orientals, and their turbaned chief Fedallah becomes Ahab's constant companion on the voyage. Fedallah, "a creature as civilized, domestic people in the temperate zone only see in their dreams, and that but dimly; but the like of whom now and then glide among the unchanging Asiatic communities" (230), is a Parsee.[4] With these mysterious stowaways as acolytes, Ahab participates in several pseudoreligious ceremonies: the perverted sacrament of the harpoons, the fashioning of a special harpoon in the fiery forge and the baptizing of it with blood, and the defiant worship of the lightning that strikes the *Pequod*. These events, together with the men who surround Ahab, show him set apart from God's world and "far gone . . . in the dark side of earth" (520-21).

Overbearing pride is the key to Ahab's character. He is proud of his own authority and enraged that anyone has authority over him. Every act of his defiance is motivated by his pride, even when he claims to be acting humanely or driven by fate. When he defies the lightning that strikes the *Pequod,* he compares its power to his own: "Light though thou be, thou leapest out of darkness; but I am darkness leaping out of light, leaping out of thee! . . . defyingly I worship thee!" (500-501). Deliberately Ahab chooses to put his own power above that of the lightning (and later the wind) and to stress his own nobility in comparison to them. Ahab's similarity to Milton's Satan, which has often been noted, involves chiefly the fatal pride of the two characters; and Ahab also fancies himself as something of a Prometheus, although Ahab's defiance of God, motivated by pride, seeks to elevate Ahab's stature rather than to aid a struggling mankind. For example, when Ahab takes the Negro boy Pip in his personal charge after Pip's experience overboard has driven him mad, Ahab makes a great show of human sympathy: "Oh, ye frozen heavens! look down here. Ye did beget

4. The Parsees, a remnant of the ancient Persian Zoroastrians, are India's fire-worshipping sect. Useful notes on "Fedallah" and "fire-worship" in the Hendricks House edition discuss the significance of Ahab's Asiatic alter ego and cite other relevant studies.

this luckless child, and have abandoned him, ye creative libertines. Here, boy; Ahab's cabin shall be Pip's home henceforth. . . ." (514). Ahab then calls to the crew: "Lo! ye believers in gods all goodness, and in man all ill, lo you! see the omniscient gods oblivious of suffering man; and man . . . full of the sweet things of love and gratitude. Come! I feel prouder leading thee by thy black hand, than though I grasped an Emperor's!" (515). The last sentence is a clue to an important motive in Ahab's befriending of Pip. Of course Ahab's recognition of his own madness draws him emotionally to the maddened Pip. There is a sympathetic identification: Ahab sees both himself and Pip as playthings of the heavenly libertines. Yet however tempting it may be to discern feelings of humanity and charity alone in Ahab's overtures to the Negro boy—and such appearances Ahab is deliberately cultivating—another strong motivation lies elsewhere. Ahab's actions spring not alone out of sympathy, but also out of his need to boost his ego by playing a humane role when he believes the gods are indifferent.

Ahab's pride is at the root of his monomania. When his ivory leg is splintered by the crashing Moby Dick, he reveals how deeply his physical debility has scarred him. The artificial leg has been shattered, rendering him virtually helpless, and it humiliates him to require Starbuck's assistance to reach the deck of the ship. "Oh, oh, oh! how this splinter gores me now! Accursed fate! that the unconquerable captain in the soul should have such a craven mate!" (552-53). Starbuck at first thinks he is the mate referred to, but Ahab quickly shouts that he is thinking of his own body, the mate to his soul. Ahab shows that his spirit of defiance, an outward manifestation of what he believes is his unconquerable soul, is a compensation for the humiliation of a shattered body. At the same time he is pleased that the ivory leg is not part of the real Ahab: "Nor white whale, nor man, nor fiend, can so much as graze old Ahab in his own proper and inaccessible being" (552).

Ahab's last speech is a climax of his proud defiance. With

45

the *Pequod* and its crew sinking in the swirling water, Ahab knows that his end has come. Yet he is "cut off from the last fond pride of meanest shipwrecked captains" (565), the honor of going down with his ship. His death is a lonely death, culminating a lonely life, but he still has the courage and the pride to face defiantly its humiliation: "Oh, now I feel my topmost greatness lies in my topmost grief. . . . Towards thee I roll, thou all-destroying but unconquering whale; to the last I grapple with thee; from hell's heart I stab at thee; for hate's sake I spit my last breath at thee" (565). In his fierce pride Ahab believes himself to be unconquered though he is destroyed. The depth of Ahab's character, revealed by a great art, makes him a figure of Satanic proportions. More than a symbol of a captain's authority, Ahab has proudly and consciously assumed whatever authority derives from the power of the evil will. The possessor of this kind of dark authority, invested with demonic power, transcends the world of human experience ("grand, ungodly, god-like man") and ultimately finds himself in opposition to the authority of God.[5]

Because of his desire to discover the secrets of the white whale, Ishmael has nominally submitted to Captain Ahab's authority, but he still remains apart from Ahab's monomaniacal pursuit and ultimately recognizes it for what it is. Interwoven with Captain Ahab's blasphemous defiance of God's authority are Ishmael's revelations concerning his own status in the hunt for Moby Dick. All the matters hinted in Ishmael's characterization of himself in the first chapter are expanded during the course of the voyage. As a roving outcast, for example, Ishmael has moved farther into exile from Christendom on the *Pequod*. The business of whaling itself

5. Bernstein, by way of contrast, emphasizes the intelligent malignity of the white whale and therefore concludes: "Ahab has the most profound vision of life of any character in the novel, and his vision of the whale, while oversimplified, is the best single evaluation of Moby-Dick" (p. 107). And later: "Ahab's way is the way of madness and destruction, but it is also the way of strength and honesty. Though Ahab's philosophy is inevitably suicidal, there is no question that Melville's sympathies lie with the *Pequod*'s captain" (pp. 124-25).

isolates men from civilization, and serving under a captain like Ahab makes the withdrawal more complete. Ishmael again points out that going to sea is much like committing suicide, for "Death is only a launching into the region of the strange Untried; it is but the first salutation to the possibilities of the immense Remote, the Wild, the Watery, the Unshored" (481), just as is whaling. There is a sadness, according to Ishmael, in going to sea; for the ocean, "which is the dark side of this earth" (422), represents for him the vast part of man's experience that God's sun does not illumine. Because two-thirds of this earth is characterized by such darkness, and because men like Ahab strive there, the mortal man who has more joy than sorrow is either not true to himself or he is immature. The greatest sadness for Ishmael is that life's secrets seem to be revealed only in the grave: "Our souls are like those orphans whose unwedded mothers die in bearing them: the secret of our paternity lies in their grave, and we must there to learn it" (487). Inasmuch as going to sea has some of the finality of death, Ishmael hopes to fathom at least part of the mystery on this voyage. It is in this frame of mind that Ishmael observes Captain Ahab's pursuit of the white whale.

When Ishmael discusses Captain Ahab's vengeful hunt for Moby Dick, more is revealed about Ahab than about the whale itself. Ishmael tells about Ahab's first disastrous encounter with the whale and remarks that "no turbaned Turk, no hired Venetian or Malay, could have smote him with more seeming malice" (181). The word *seeming* in Ishmael's account is important. Ishmael does not here ascribe malice to the whale, but indicates rather that so it seemed to Ahab. The result was that "his torn body and gashed soul bled into one another; and so interfusing, made him mad" (182). Certainly there is sympathy in Ishmael's characterization of Ahab. Ahab is a man who feels malicious agencies at work in him; Ishmael feels such stirrings himself. But it is madness, as Ishmael so states, to be moved to a wild, vindictive monomania by intellectual and spiritual exasperations. While Ish-

47

mael does have a vital interest in discovering the secrets of the white whale, he does not impute the same evil to Moby Dick, the same malice and intelligent malignity, that motivates Ahab. On the contrary, Ishmael feels pity for his captain: "God help thee, old man, thy thoughts have created a creature in thee; and he whose intense thinking thus makes him a Prometheus; a vulture feeds upon that heart forever; that vulture the very creature he creates" (200). Only once is Ishmael drawn up by enthusiasm into Ahab's feud with Moby Dick. It occurs when the sailors gather before the mast and pledge death to Moby Dick with the liquor drunk from the hollow of the harpoons. This ceremony affects Ishmael as it does the other members of the crew: "I, Ishmael, was one of that crew; my shouts had gone up with the rest; my oath had been welded with theirs; and stronger I shouted, and more did I hammer and clinch my oath, because of the dread in my soul. A wild, mystical, sympathetical feeling was in me. Ahab's quenchless feud seemed mine" (175). Ishmael's enthusiasm, engendered by the emotion of the occasion and fortified by a strong draught of liquor, proves to be only temporary. In a calmer and more sober mood soon thereafter he realizes that "while yet all a-rush to encounter the whale," still he "could see naught in that brute but the deadliest ill" (185). Months later, while at work in the try-works with his hands deep in sperm oil, Ishmael forgets all about his "horrible oath," remarking that perhaps sperm oil has a "rare virtue in allaying the heat of anger," because he feels "divinely free from all ill-will, or petulance, or malice, of any sort whatsoever" (414). It has taken him a long time to recover completely from the spirit of vengeance that infected him at Ahab's ceremony, but he has recovered. Furthermore, the very wording of his statement indicates the change: he is divinely free from malice. The implication is the exact opposite of Ahab's belief in divine malice, which imputes to God human qualities.

Chapter XLII of *Moby-Dick*, entitled "The Whiteness of the Whale," is the thematic center of the novel. In this chapter Ishmael explains to the reader what the white whale means to him. The importance of the chapter is stressed by Ishmael in its opening sentence: "What the white whale was to Ahab, has been hinted; what, at times, he was to me, as yet remains unsaid" (185). Such a beginning not only serves to emphasize the importance of what is to come, but also effectively separates Ishmael (and Melville) from what has already been related, much of it in the immediately preceding chapter, about Ahab's beliefs. In his explanation of the whale's color Ishmael first turns to what might be called the "good" associations man has with whiteness: the beauty of white marbles and pearls, the royal pre-eminence of white elephants and white chargers, the joyfulness signified by the white stone in Roman times, the benignity of white hair, the majesty of judges in white ermine, the sacredness of white vestures in religious ceremonies, and so on. These are only a few of the examples Ishmael cites of the association man has between whiteness and "whatever is sweet, and honorable, and sublime" (186). Next he turns to what might be termed the "evil" associations man has with whiteness: the white bear, the white shark, the mingled worship and horror of the legendary white steed of the prairies, the hideous albino of every species, the marble pallor of the dead, the hue of the shroud, the whiteness of ghosts, and so on. There is an elusive quality in whiteness that causes it, when "coupled with any object terrible in itself, to heighten that terror to the furthest bounds" (186). The important problem, according to Ishmael, is therefore to explain the duality of whiteness, the good and evil of it. He continues with many more examples drawn from both aspects of whiteness, and then he admits near the end of the chapter: "But not yet have we solved the incantation of this whiteness, and learned why it appeals with such power to the soul; and more strange and far more portentous —why, as we have seen, it is at once the most meaning symbol of spiritual things, nay, the very veil of the Christian's Deity; and yet should be as it is, the intensifying agent in things the most appalling to mankind" (193). Ishmael's answer comes in the form of two questions: "Is it that by its indefiniteness it shadows forth the heartless voids and immensities of the universe, and thus stabs us from behind with the thought of annihilation. . . . Or is it, that as in essence whiteness is not so much a color as the visible absence of color, and at the same time the concrete of all colors . . . that there is such a dumb blankness, full of meaning. . . ." (193).

These are suggestions rather than answers. Ishmael admits that the hue of divine whiteness is virtually inexplicable, that only the imaginative man can grasp but dimly its meaning. Whiteness "shadows forth"—i.e., represents faintly and mystically—the heartless voids and immensities of the universe. Knowledge is based upon predicates, that which is affirmed or denied of a subject. But what can be predicated of this faint and mystical hue? Reflecting all the rays of the spectrum combined, whiteness is at once the visible presence and absence of color. In short, whiteness is inscrutable, the veil of God. When man perceives whiteness he may be appalled, because the divine intensifying agent evokes awe and terror; or he may feel a sweet, mystical sublimity. It would seem that the response would depend partly, though not entirely, upon man's own consciousness. God has created the world and drawn a veil of inscrutability over good and evil. That the two are inextricable is part of the mystery, just as the interwoven strands of fate, free will, and chance cannot be unraveled by man. Man cannot fathom the mystery because he cannot penetrate the veil, whiteness. With the authority of the Creator, God has willed it so. Captain Ahab, who is obsessed with the idea that maliciousness motivated God to so construct the world, pursues Moby Dick with defiant anger. Ishmael joins the hunt for the white whale in the hope of discovering its secret mysteries. Once the centrality of the Ishmael-Ahab-Moby Dick relationship is understood, the peripheral matters that have a bearing on the theme can be profitably examined.

The sermon of Father Mapple, which Ishmael hears in the New Bedford whaleman's chapel before he joins the *Pequod* in Nantucket, is the structural metaphor that foreshadows and illuminates the entire subsequent action of the book.

50

Father Mapple's mild appearance and humble bearing stand in contrast to Captain Ahab. When the chaplain ascends the rope ladder to his pulpit and draws it up behind him, Ishmael ascribes to the act a symbolic significance, for "by that act of physical isolation, he signifies his spiritual withdrawal for the time, from all outward worldly ties and connections" (38). By calling attention to this detail, Ishmael indicates a contrast between Mapple and Ahab. The chaplain withdraws from worldly ties, Ahab from the Christian world. Father Mapple's withdrawal is for the purpose of purification and sanctification, while Ahab's isolation is motivated by a rejection of Christian brotherhood. Father Mapple seems to enter upon an upward, spiritual journey of ascension, Ahab to withdraw into his own hell. The contrast is further illustrated when Father Mapple begins to speak "in a mild voice of unassuming authority" (39). Even as the pilot of God, the chaplain's voice is one of Christian humility.

Father Mapple takes as his text for his sermon the story of Jonah and the whale. He announces to his congregation that the Book of Jonah contains two lessons: "a lesson to us all as sinful men, and a lesson to me as a pilot of the living God" (41). The lesson to all men is that Jonah's sin consisted of "his wilful disobedience of the command of God" (41). Ahab is, of course, the chief example in the book of this sin. Father Mapple then proceeds to relate the story of Jonah with appropriate nautical interpolations. At the end of his ordeal Jonah prays to the Lord and is delivered out of the whale's belly. Father Mapple draws this conclusion: "Sin not; but if you do, take heed to repent of it like Jonah" (46). The elements of humility, repentance, and acceptance in Jonah's story stand in contrast to Captain Ahab's pride, anger, and defiance.

The second part of Father Mapple's conclusion, the lesson to himself as a chaplain, seems also applicable to Ishmael. Mapple points out that Jonah had fled from the sight of the Lord because he had been unwilling to preach, as an appointed pilot-prophet, the "unwelcome truths in the ears of a wicked Nineveh" (47). Jonah had been unable to escape the power

51

of God, and in the end he did God's bidding: "To preach the Truth to the face of Falsehood!" (47). So Father Mapple extracts his second lesson from the story: "This, shipmates, this is that other lesson; and woe to that pilot of the living God who slights it. Woe to him whom this world charms from Gospel duty! Woe to him who seeks to pour oil upon the waters when God has brewed them into a gale! Woe to him who seeks to please rather than to appal! . . . Yea, woe to him who, as the great Pilot Paul has it, while preaching to others is himself a castaway!" (47). The second lesson may well apply to Ishmael as well as to Father Mapple himself. It would not be incompatible with Melville's view of the vocation of the writer as artist and thinker to equate it with that of the preacher: each is a pilot-prophet. Ishmael's task at hand is to observe and to narrate the terrible story of Captain Ahab, the true telling of which imposes certain responsibilities. It may be that something of the agony of the writer is implicit in this sermon about the call to "gospel duty." Passion, melancholy, cynicism, even an unthinking easy acceptance—any of these human attitudes, perhaps malice above all, might turn Ishmael aside from his duty to the truth. He must guard against emphasizing Ahab's stature and authority and minimizing the wrath of God. However unpleasant is God's authority, however appalling to man, he must reveal the inexorable nature of God's decrees. Furthermore, Ishmael himself must accept the authority of God while demonstrating it to others, and he must cease to be a castaway. If Ishmael will do all these things, Father Mapple assures him of the "top-gallant delight" (48) of salvation.[6]

The requirements for Ishmael's salvation are not easy to fulfill. The structure of the book demands that Ishmael never oppose Ahab by overt action or speech: he is witness, recorder, and reporter. In the entire novel there is never a conversation recorded between Ishmael and Ahab. Ishmael's role as per-

6. Bernstein avers that "the type of delight mentioned by Father Mapple is a delusion and a mockery, for it is unattainable by man" (p. 93).

ceptive bystander springs from the nature of his character and the intensity of his thoughts. In telling Ahab's story he does succeed in demonstrating the appalling wrath of God, a jealous wrath that finally wraps up men (good, bad, and indifferent) and timbers in the great shroud of the sea. Ishmael is also successful in standing as himself against the fierce Ahab, one of those whom Father Mapple has labeled the "proud gods and commodores of this earth" (48), because Ishmael does not allow Ahab except for a brief time to enlist his soul and spirit in the venture. That Ishmael is successful in these two ways is shown by the fact that he survives the fury of Moby Dick and the final wreck of the *Pequod*. One attendant benefit of standing apart from Ahab, who sees nobility in his own isolation, is Ishmael's achievement of a good relationship with Queequeg. The humanity and brotherhood growing out of their friendship seems to be unique aboard the *Pequod* and gives another thematic relevancy to Ishmael's survival.[7] Yet by going on the voyage as a common sailor, which deliberately precludes any office of authority and any responsibility, and by never intervening to bring his insight into Ahab's demonic character to the others—to this extent Ishmael fails Father Mapple's test. And because Ishmael cannot quite bring himself to leave the mystery of eternity to God, he remains in the end still a castaway, and thus a measure of woe remains to him.

Starbuck, the chief mate of the *Pequod*, brings to the novel the orthodox Christian attitude toward Ahab's pursuit of the white whale. Ishmael describes Starbuck as an earnest man, of hardy sobriety and fortitude, endowed with a deep, natural reverence. Starbuck soon becomes aware of the true nature of Ahab's hunt and its menacing implications for the *Pequod's* crew. Ishmael's way of saying that Starbuck is a religious

7. For an excellent discussion of the thematic reasons for Ishmael's survival and the Ishmael-Bulkington-Queequeg relationship, see William Rosenfeld, "Uncertain Faith: Queequeg's Coffin and Melville's Use of the Bible," *Texas Studies in Language and Literature*, VII (Winter 1966), 317-27.

man is to remark that Starbuck is strongly inclined toward superstition, "but to that sort of superstition, which in some organizations seems rather to spring, somehow, from intelligence than from ignorance" (112). This characterization is relatively kind when Melville's own rebellion against orthodox religious forms is recalled. The emphasis on the superstitious nature of orthodoxy is not surprising, but it is a superstition of the highest form, which, springing from intelligence, might be called faith. Ishmael does not accept for himself this orthodoxy, but neither does he spurn Starbuck for doing so. The weakness, as Ishmael points out, in Starbuck's intrepid bravery, is that "while generally abiding firm in the conflict with seas, or winds, or whales, or any of the ordinary irrational horrors of the world," yet it "cannot withstand those more terrific, because more spiritual terrors, which sometimes menace you from the concentrating brow of an enraged and mighty man" (113). Perhaps this is to say that it is difficult for orthodoxy to cope with the pride of the evil will. More specifically, the tragedy of Starbuck is that he is not strong enough completely and finally to stand apart from Captain Ahab and defy his authority. It will be remembered that to stand apart from the proud gods of the earth was one of Father Mapple's tests for the faithful Christian. This is the test that Starbuck ultimately fails.

During the blasphemous ceremony that Ahab conducts at the *Pequod*'s mast, Starbuck alone raises a voice in protest. Except for Ishmael, only Starbuck seems aware of the diabolical nature of the ceremony. When Ahab cries for vengeance on Moby Dick, Starbuck makes his protest heard by the crew: "Vengeance on a dumb brute! . . . that simply smote thee from blindest instinct! Madness! To be enraged with a dumb thing, Captain Ahab, seems blasphemous" (161). Captain Ahab cannot ignore his chief mate, and so he directs a long speech at Starbuck that is intended to justify Ahab's desire for revenge and placate his subordinate. Alternately flushing and turning pale, Starbuck stares dumbly at his captain, but he does not speak up again when Ahab invites him to do so. Ahab is jubilant, and Starbuck can only murmur lowly, "God keep me!—keep us all!" as Ahab turns away "in his joy at the enchanted, tacit acquiescence" (162) of his mate. Starbuck has been enchanted by the wizard-like Ahab, and his courage fails him in his first test with his captain. Though inwardly Starbuck rebels, his years at sea have formed in him such a strong habit of obedience to his captain that he cannot at that moment translate the inward rebellion into speech or action. As Ahab knows, Starbuck is now trapped; for his failure to protest vigorously Ahab's first revelation of his purpose means that overt opposition in the future can be construed as mutiny.

The scene that pictures Starbuck alone after his failure at the diabolical ceremony shows him sick of heart and soul. Unlike Ishmael, who found himself caught up with enthusiasm for the hunt, Starbuck deplores what is happening to himself and the others: "My soul is more than matched; she's over-manned; and by a madman! . . . I think I see his impious end; but feel that I must help him to it. . . . Oh! I plainly see my miserable office,—to obey, rebelling; and worse yet, to hate with touch of pity!" (166-67). At this moment Starbuck realizes what the end to the hunt must be; at the same time he knows how inexorably Ahab's authority coerces all of them. Ahab's mesmerizing power has overwhelmed Starbuck, because cogent thinking on his part would force him to the conclusion that his only salvation lies in opposing Ahab. Pity also clouds the mind of the chief mate, and it is, after all, a mind that is not characterized as incisive. Starbuck ends this scene by expressing the weak hope that Ahab will not find Moby Dick in the vast expanse of the ocean and thus the catastrophe will be averted.

As the voyage progresses, Captain Ahab shrewdly perceives the limits of his authority over Starbuck, while at the same time he takes full advantage of his mate's acquiescence. It is partly to pacify Starbuck that Ahab distracts the crew with the ordinary business of taking whales despite his own impatience. Both of them see the crew's restlessness, and

Starbuck seems to have been gathering courage for another protest. Ahab knows that "the chief mate, in his soul, abhorred his captain's quest, and could he, would joyfully disintegrate himself from it, or even frustrate it" (210). Ahab also takes advantage of Starbuck's disapproving attitude, which is known to the crew, as a means of pacifying the ordinary sailors. The men are vaguely concerned with the impious nature of Ahab's vengeance, but they know Starbuck to be a staunchly Christian man. Ahab is shrewd enough to realize that if he can maintain in his chief mate at least a tacit acquiescence, the sailors will accord all the ship's officers their obedience without further thought. Ishmael shows his own awareness of this situation when he remarks that the sailors were "morally enfeebled . . . by the incompetence of mere unaided virtue or right-mindedness in Starbuck" (184).

Starbuck believes that it is his responsibility to extricate himself and the crew from the tangled web of Captain Ahab's authority. His dilemma is that on the one hand he knows himself to be the most powerful force for good on the *Pequod*, and on the other hand as second in command of the ship he is bound to uphold his captain's authority. Starbuck's solution offers little more chance of success than the vain hope that Ahab will fail to find Moby Dick: he tries to persuade Ahab to give up the hunt and return home. He is still trying on that final day when the ship is smashed and all of them (except Ishmael) are drowned. An early occasion for Starbuck to speak out arises when the lightning strikes the *Pequod* and Ahab worships it defiantly. During that incident Starbuck grasps Ahab by the arm and pleads with him: "God, God is against thee, old man; forbear! 'tis an ill voyage! ill begun, ill continued; let me square the yards, while we may, old man, and make a fair wind of it homewards, to go on a better voyage than this" (501). Starbuck's plea is partly responsible for the crew's sudden panic, and Ahab is forced to remind them of their sworn oaths in order to restore his control over them.

Soon after this incident, Starbuck happens to enter the

56

captain's cabin at night when Ahab is sleeping. The mate sees a loaded musket in its rack, and for a brief moment Starbuck toys with the idea of murdering Ahab while he sleeps. Starbuck's hands shake in this horrifying moment of decision, but for him cold-blooded murder, even of this madman who is leading them all to destruction, is impossible. Starbuck realizes that neither reasoning, remonstrance, nor entreaty will sway Ahab from his purpose. There in the cabin Starbuck tries to think of a lawful way of deposing the captain. He considers taking him prisoner, but rejects that as impractical because wresting Ahab's power from him would be difficult and containing him on the voyage home virtually impossible. Starbuck realizes that the *Pequod*'s isolation from civilization puts two oceans and a continent between the ship and the law. Despairingly, Starbuck leaves the cabin without Ahab's ever realizing that he has been there. Captain Ahab sleeps securely in the confident knowledge that he need fear no physical violence from his chief mate.

Because of Starbuck's secret visit to the captain's cabin, a later incident becomes invested with heavy irony. It develops that when Captain Ahab later wants to swing himself in a looped line and be hoisted to the masthead to scout for Moby Dick, it is Starbuck whom he selects to secure the loose end of the rope and stand guard over it while Ahab perches at the top. Ahab rejects his pagan harpooners and his chief wizard Fedallah for that duty. The captain knows only too well the character of each of the men in his command. Starbuck, then, knows that his powers of persuasion have failed and that other methods of relief are impractical, but his own personal qualities and principles prevent him from justifying the act of murder as a means to attain a moral end. Nothing he can do to oppose Ahab's authority is effective.

In the last frantic days of the *Pequod,* Starbuck repeatedly renews his futile pleas with Ahab to desist from the hunt. After the second day of the chase when Ahab's ivory leg is splintered, Starbuck pleads in vain: "Shall we keep chasing this murderous fish till he swamps the last man? Shall we be dragged by him to the bottom of the sea? Shall we be towed by him to the infernal world? Oh, oh,—Impiety and blasphemy to hunt him more!" (553). On the climactic third day of the chase, Starbuck weeps as he makes his final plea on the deck of the *Pequod*: "Oh, my captain, my captain!—noble heart—go not—go not!—see, it's a brave man that weeps; how great the agony of the persuasion then!" (558). Ahab turns to lower his boat, and Starbuck agrees to keep the ship close to the fray, although he says: "I misdoubt me that I disobey my God in obeying him!" (557). When Moby Dick turns on the *Pequod*, Starbuck calls on his God: "Is this the end of all my bursting prayers? all my life-long fidelities? Oh, Ahab, Ahab, lo, thy work. Steady! helmsman, steady. Nay, nay! Up helm again! He turns to meet us! Oh, his unappeasable brow drives on towards one, whose duty tells him he cannot depart. My God, stand by me now!" (564). The ship is doomed. Ishmael describes the whale's wrath: "Retribution, swift vengeance, eternal malice were in his whole aspect, and spite of all that mortal man could do, the solid white buttress of his forehead smote the ship's starboard bow, till men and timbers reeled" (564-65). This description contains the only words by Ishmael in the novel that seem to ascribe malice to the whale, and even here the phrase "in his whole aspect" may indicate that the malice is more apparent than real. Obviously Moby Dick has now good reason to be enraged by his pursuers. Because of Ahab's work, Starbuck's prayer to God is futile.

Starbuck's unique position aboard the *Pequod* serves to crystallize the theme of authority in *Moby-Dick*.[8] The chief mate brings an attitude representing orthodox Christianity to a ship commanded by a captain engaged in a blasphemous

8. Here I am in agreement with Bernstein's statement that Starbuck and Ahab represent "the two major conflicting philosophies of the book" (p. 93). I do not share, however, Bernstein's conclusion about Starbuck's philosophy: "But, as developed in *Moby-Dick*, this philosophy is not only weak, but it is essentially dishonest, for it is based on a false premise. All evidence indicates that the universe is not governed by forces sympathetic to man" (p. 124).

mission. Starbuck is thus torn between the two aspects of authority that are of paramount importance in the novel: the authority of Captain Ahab and the authority of God. Starbuck must make a choice because he cannot serve both God and Ahab, and he understands the alternatives when he states that he disobeys God when he obeys Ahab. Before that he has tried to compromise by acquiescing in his captain's demands and at the same time registering inward protest. He justifies this compromise by protesting aloud to Ahab when he has the opportunity and by praying that Ahab will not find Moby Dick. Unfortunately, Starbuck's outward compliance furthers Ahab's purpose by allaying the fears of the crew. By the time Starbuck realizes that his position between the authority of his captain and the authority of his God is untenable, it is too late. The attitude he brings to the *Pequod,* his subsequent actions, and his ultimate failure cause the theme of authority to assume a fixed and definite form.

Upon Ishmael alone, however, depends the resolution of the theme. Melville's narrator has literally embarked upon a voyage of discovery in which he hopes to learn the secrets of God, concealed by the depths of the ocean and symbolized by the white whale. Each revelation of the first chapter concerning the nature of his quest is consistently developed as the voyage progresses. The sea continues to represent for him the "inscrutable tides of God" (157). Repeatedly he underlines the importance of his quest and its dangerous implications: "But in pursuit of those far mysteries we dream of, or in tormented chase of that demon phantom that, some time or other, swims before all human hearts; while chasing such over this round globe, they either lead us on in barren mazes or midway leave us whelmed" (236). The secure ease of life on shore is not for Ishmael. He develops at great length the contrast between the security of the land and the adventure of the sea. The analogy applies to the dual portions of man's consciousness as well as to his outside world, "for as this appalling ocean surrounds the verdant land, so in the soul of man there lies one insular Tahiti, full of peace and

59

joy, but encompassed by all the horrors of the half known life" (274). While Ishmael admits that greater happiness may lie for some in the mild joy of the insular life, greater satisfaction comes to him when launching into unknown waters. Such is the destiny of the wandering Ishmael. His temporary allegiance to the authority of Captain Ahab is a means by which he hopes to discover the meaning of a higher authority. Ishmael's aim, as indicated by his discussion of the whiteness of the whale, is to draw aside the veil of God. When Captain Ahab cries vengeance and attacks Moby Dick, Ishmael is not, finally, a participant. Nor can Ishmael accept the prayerful, seemingly powerless, orthodox faith of Starbuck. He remains instead a skeptic: "Doubts of all things earthly, and intuitions of some things heavenly; this combination makes neither believer nor infidel, but makes a man who regards them both with equal eye" (372). Ishmael regards the struggle between Ahab and Starbuck with an equal eye, hoping to discover in the end why the Creator made such men, put them in such a world, and concealed His work in mystery.

Ishmael's voyage of discovery does not provide him with the answers he seeks. The swift retribution of Moby Dick destroys both the defiant Ahab and the prayerful Starbuck, and the white whale escapes Ishmael. It happens because God, with the authority of the Creator, has so willed it. Good and evil men alike perish by His wrath, and the import of the novel is that the authority of God is inscrutable.[9] Over the sinking ship and the fleeing whale "the great shroud of

9. Leon F. Seltzer, "Camus's Absurd and the World of Melville's *Confidence-Man*," *PMLA*, LXXXII (March, 1967), 22, writes: "While the author might continue to feel rebellious toward the mysterious forces that doomed his quest for rational knowledge, in *The Confidence-Man*, for the very first time he shows himself willing to employ his art to demonstrate systematically his (and, by extension, every man's) innate incapacity to comprehend the universe objectively." Although *Moby-Dick* may not be as "systematic" in its demonstration of this idea as *The Confidence-Man*, and certainly the focus of the earlier work is broader, it seems to me precisely this conclusion that Melville does demonstrate in *Moby-Dick*.

the sea rolled on as it rolled five thousand years ago" (566). The narrative has come full circle, and once again, this time literally, Ishmael is adrift. He is rescued and returned physically to the society of men by the cruising *Rachel, "that in her retracing search after her missing children, only found another orphan"* (567), but spiritually he remains a castaway. *Moby-Dick* begins and ends with Ishmael, the roving orphan whose adventure at sea fails to put him any nearer to an understanding of the ungraspable phantom of life. It is not in this life that the mystery of God's authority is to be revealed. The secret of the orphan's paternity lies in the grave.

Thus Melville's romances and novels through 1851 reveal a mind shrewdly perceptive of the nature of authority and discerning of its function. The authority of church, state, and society is the framework within which Melville's sailor-narrator operates in the early romances. The authority of the ship captain is derived through law and custom from the authority of the state, and it is, of course, immediately and intensely of interest to a sailor. The question continually posed in these works is whether the authority is vested in fact by warrant of moral right or is being used under that guise for the selfish interests of men and institutions. Depending upon the answer, Melville ranges in his attitude from a rather begrudging acceptance to outright rebellion.

By 1851 Melville's interest turns to the all-embracing concept of the authority of God. Since the lesser authorities claim sanction from this higher one, *Moby-Dick* summarizes the treatment of the theme in the earlier works. To Captain Ahab, whose drama Ishmael presents to us, the mysterious authority of God is tinged with malice. Ahab responds to this seeming malice with a rage at once proud and defiant, and thus he begets his own destruction. Ishmael and Melville are left with the inscrutable—the veil of whiteness—and, covering all, the great shroud of the sea.

UNIVERSITY OF FLORIDA MONOGRAPHS

Humanities

No. 1: *Uncollected Letters of James Gates Percival*, edited by Harry R. Warfel

No. 2: *Leigh Hunt's Autobiography: The Earliest Sketches*, edited by Stephen F. Fogle

No. 3: *Pause Patterns in Elizabethan and Jacobean Drama*, by Ants Oras

No. 4: *Rhetoric and American Poetry of the Early National Period*, by Gordon E. Bigelow

No. 5: *The Background of The Princess Casamassima*, by W. H. Tilley

No. 6: *Indian Sculpture in the John and Mable Ringling Museum of Art*, by Roy C. Craven, Jr.

No. 7: *The Cestus. A Mask*, edited by Thomas B. Stroup

No. 8: *Tamburlaine, Part I, and Its Audience*, by Frank B. Fieler

No. 9: *The Case of John Darrell: Minister and Exorcist*, by Corinne Holt Rickert

No. 10: *Reflections of the Civil War in Southern Humor*, by Wade H. Hall

No. 11: *Charles Dodgson, Semeiotician*, by Daniel F. Kirk

No. 12: *Three Middle English Religious Poems*, edited by R. H. Bowers

No. 13: *The Existentialism of Miguel de Unamuno*, by José Huertas-Jourda

No. 14: *Four Spiritual Crises in Mid-Century American Fiction*, by Robert Detweiler

No. 15: *Style and Society in German Literary Expressionism*, by Egbert Krispyn

No. 16: *The Reach of Art: A Study in the Prosody of Pope*, by Jacob H. Adler

No. 17: *Malraux, Sartre, and Aragon as Political Novelists*, by Catharine Savage

No. 18: *Las Guerras Carlistas y el Reinado Isabelino en la Obra de Ramón del Valle-Inclán*, por María Dolores Lado

No. 19: *Diderot's Vie de Sénèque: A Swan Song Revised*, by Douglas A. Bonneville

No. 20: *Blank Verse and Chronology in Milton* by Ants Oras

No. 21: *Milton's Elisions*, by Robert O. Evans

No. 22: *Prayer in Sixteenth-Century England*, by Faye L. Kelly

No. 23: *The Strangers: The Tragic World of Tristan L'Hermite*, by Claude K. Abraham

No. 24: *Dramatic Uses of Biblical Allusion in Marlowe and Shakespeare*, by James H. Sims

No. 25: *Doubt and Dogma in Maria Edgeworth*, by Mark D. Hawthorne

No. 26: *The Masses of Francesco Soriano*, by S. Philip Kniseley

No. 27: *Love as Death in The Iceman Cometh*, by Winifred Dusenbury Frazer

No. 28: *Melville and Authority*, by Nicholas Canaday, Jr.